Deleuze's
Bergsonism

To my two great mentors in matters Bergson and Deleuze,
Robin Durie and Paul Patton.

Deleuze's Bergsonism

CRAIG LUNDY

EDINBURGH
University Press

Edinburgh University Press is one of the leading university presses in the UK. We publish academic books and journals in our selected subject areas across the humanities and social sciences, combining cutting-edge scholarship with high editorial and production values to produce academic works of lasting importance. For more information visit our website: edinburghuniversitypress.com

Edinburgh University Press Ltd
The Tun – Holyrood Road
12(2f) Jackson's Entry
Edinburgh EH8 8PJ

Typeset in 11.5/15 Adobe Sabon by
IDSUK (DataConnection) Ltd, and
printed and bound in Great Britain.

A CIP record for this book is available from the British Library

ISBN 978 1 4744 1430 2 (hardback)
ISBN 978 1 4744 1433 3 (webready PDF)
ISBN 978 1 4744 1431 9 (paperback)
ISBN 978 1 4744 1432 6 (epub)

Contents

Acknowledgements

This book has its origin in two reading groups that I attended as a student, which explored the work of Bergson and Deleuze – one organised by Robin Durie in Exeter, and the other by Paul Patton in Sydney. It was in these groups that I learnt what it meant to read a text properly. I therefore have much to thank Robin and Paul for: their pedagogical practice, insights on Bergson/Deleuze, professional advice, and last but not least, friendship. Along the way I have had countless discussions and debates about matters Bergson and Deleuze that have all fed into this book. While it is impossible to cite all my interlocutors here, please forgive me for singling out the following: Nadine Boljkovac, Sean Bowden, Ian Buchanan, Simon Duffy, Gregg Flaxman, Mike Hale, Joe Hughes, Masa Kosugi, Gregg Lambert, John Ó Maoilearca, Jon Roffe, Anne Sauvagnargues, Henry Somers-Hall, Dan Smith, Marcelo Svirsky, Iris van der Tuin, Daniela Voss, Nathan Widder and James Williams. Much credit for this book must also go to Carol Macdonald, who approached me about writing a monograph of this kind. At the time it had not been my intention to do so, but as those who know Carol will confirm, she is a difficult person to say no to, for all the best reasons. Needless to say I have found her work and that of the team at EUP to be nothing short of outstanding. Finally, I must thank Stevie Voogt, though the term 'thanks'

vii

hardly approaches how I feel and what she deserves. Since taking on this project we have experienced several momentous life changes, and through it all she has shouldered much of the weight whilst also being my support. This book is thus as much hers as it is anyone's, so I hope that I've done it justice.

Abbreviations

Bergson

CE   *Creative Evolution*, trans. Arthur Mitchell. Mineola, NY: Dover, [1907] 1998.

CM   *The Creative Mind: An Introduction to Metaphysics*, trans. Mabelle L. Andison. Mineola, NY: Dover, [1934] 2007.

DS   *Duration and Simultaneity: Bergson and the Einsteinian Universe*, ed. Robin Durie. Manchester: Clinamen Press, [1922] 1999.

ME   *Mind-Energy*, trans. H. Wildon Carr. Basingstoke: Palgrave Macmillan, [1919] 2007.

MM   *Matter and Memory,* trans. Nancy Margaret Paul and W. Scott Palmer. Mineola, NY: Dover, [1896] 2004.

TFW *Time and Free Will: An Essay on the Immediate Data of Consciousness*, trans. F. L. Pogson. Mineola, NY: Dover, [1889] 2001.

TS   *The Two Sources of Morality and Religion*, trans. R. Ashley Audra and Cloudesley Brereton. Notre Dame: University of Notre Dame Press, [1932] 1977.

Deleuze (single and co-authored)

B   *Bergsonism*, trans. Hugh Tomlinson and Barbara Habberjam. New York: Zone Books, [1966] 1991.

ix

B1   "Bergson, 1859–1941", in *Desert Islands and Other Texts: 1953–1974*, ed. David Lapoujade, trans. Michael Taormina. New York and Los Angeles: Semiotext(e), [1956] 2004.

BCD   "Bergson's Conception of Difference", in *Desert Islands and Other Texts: 1953–1974*, ed. David Lapoujade, trans. Michael Taormina. New York and Los Angeles: Semiotext(e), [1956] 2004.

C1   *Cinema 1: The Movement Image*, trans. Hugh Tomlinson and Barbara Habberjam. London: Athlone Press, [1983] 1986.

D   *Dialogues II*, co-authored with Claire Parnet, trans. Barbara Habberjam and Hugh Tomlinson. London and New York: Continuum, [1977] 2002.

DR   *Difference and Repetition*, trans. Paul Patton. London: Athlone Press, [1968] 1994.

LC   "Lecture Course on Chapter Three of Bergson's *Creative Evolution*", in *SubStance*, Issue 114, Vol. 26, No. 3, [1960] 2007, pp. 72–90.

N   *Negotiations: 1972–1990*, trans. Martin Joughin. New York: Columbia University Press, [1990] 1995.

NP   *Nietzsche and Philosophy*, trans. Hugh Tomlinson. London and New York: Continuum, [1962] 1983.

TMB   "Théorie des multiplicités chez Bergson: une conference", at www.webdeleuze.com [1970].

TRM   *Two Regimes of Madness: Texts and Interviews 1975–1995*, ed. David Lapoujade, trans. Ames Hodges and Mike Taormina. New York and Los Angeles: Semiotext(e), [2003] 2006.

Introduction

BERGSONISM LOST AND FOUND

There is a thinker whose name is today on everybody's lips, who is deemed by acknowledged philosophers worthy of comparison with the greatest, and who, with his pen as well as his brain, has overleapt all technical obstacles, and won himself a reading both outside and inside the schools. Beyond any doubt, and by common consent, Mr Henri Bergson's work will appear to future eyes among the most characteristic, fertile, and glorious of our era. It marks a never-to-be-forgotten date in history; it opens up a phase of metaphysical thought; it lays down a principle of development the limits of which are indeterminable; and it is after cool consideration, with full consciousness of the exact value of words, that we are able to pronounce the revolution which it effects equal in importance to that effected by Kant, or even by Socrates. (Edouard Le Roy, *A New Philosophy: Henri Bergson*, 1912)

Edouard Le Roy, it would appear, was not the best of fortune tellers. Future eyes did not look upon Henri Bergson so fondly. More damningly, his work was largely ignored by subsequent generations, to the point where most university students today complete their studies without once coming across Bergson's name. Le Roy was nevertheless correct about one thing when he wrote the above: in 1912, Bergson was the talk of the town. After the publication of his third book *Creative Evolution* in

1

1907, Bergson's fame rose to dizzying heights.[1] His lectures at the Collège de France became must-see events, not only for intellectuals but also for high society. As Gabriel Marcel recounts, he and others would arrive two hours early and sit through the lecture of Bergson's predecessor in the room, the political economist Paul Leroy-Beaulieu, to be sure of their seat for the main show (Marcel 1962: 124). It is also reported that servants would be sent ahead by their mistresses to reserve a place in the lecture hall (Grogin 1988: 123). Parisian periodicals recounted Bergson's lectures by comparing them to the tango, which had newly arrived in Western Europe, and fashion retailers suggested outfits in which society ladies might receive "the great metaphysician" (Grogin 1988: 175).

This fame was by no means restricted to the *à la mode* set of Paris, as illustrated by Bergson's 1913 trip to the northeast of America. For several of his lectures on this tour more than 2000 people submitted written applications for tickets (McGrath 2013: 601).[2] According to another source, at least 2000 students were present for his lecture at the City College of New York, with close to 5000 people attending one of his talks over the course of the tour (Grogin 1988: 177). To put these numbers in context, the audiences attracted by Bergson exceeded those who came to hear Sigmund Freud and Carl Jung during their 1909 trip to America (McGrath 2013: 615). So high was Bergson's reputation in America, enhanced in no small measure by the praise he received from William James and John Dewey, that come the outbreak of war in Europe Bergson was sent on two diplomatic missions by the French government to bend the ear of President Woodrow Wilson.[3] As this all suggests, for roughly a decade following the publication of *Creative Evolution* Bergson was the most celebrated intellectual in the world, with an unrivalled influence both inside and outside the academy.[4]

And yet, by the 1930s Bergson was effectively *persona non grata*. Several reasons can be given for this somewhat curious turn of events, beginning with none other than the extraordinary popularity of Bergsonism. While useful to begin with in spreading his work, Bergson's mass appeal was arguably a hindrance in the long run, for it blurred the distinction between his actual writings and a vague cultural and spiritual movement that went under the moniker 'Bergsonism'. Bergson was of course wise to the damage that his popular success could bring. In 1914 he wrote to *Le Figaro* stating: "I never made a bit of concession to the 'grand public', my teaching addresses specialists, and I have even rendered it more and more technical as the influence of my courses increases" (cited in McGrath 2013: 616–17). But despite his best efforts, it is undeniable that the enormous influence of Bergson's work outside of academia, and the resulting trivialisation of his thought, were detrimental to his intellectual legacy. As Maurice Merleau-Ponty once remarked: "Bergsonism distorts Bergson. [. . .] Bergson was a contact with things; Bergsonism is a collection of accepted opinions" (Merleau-Ponty 1962: 135).

Criticisms advanced by contemporaries of Bergson must be read with this contextual backdrop in mind. Bergson was not merely a philosopher, he was "the most dangerous man in the world" (Lippmann 1912: 100–1). Julien Benda, the self-proclaimed 'anti-Bergson', certainly felt this way, announcing that he "would happily have killed Bergson if this was the only way to destroy his influence" (Grogin 1988: ix). The vague-but-pervasive influence of Bergsonism also helps to account for why Bergson was criticised from all directions. Attacks on Bergson were mounted from the Left and the Right, the Catholic Church and Jewish intellectuals, the apostles of 'science' and defenders of philosophical tradition in the Sorbonne – "not only, then, his natural enemies, but the enemies of his enemies" (Merleau-Ponty 1962: 133).

Although the work of Julien Benda has been largely forgotten today, the same cannot be said for two of Bergson's other major critics: Bertrand Russell and Albert Einstein. Russell's unfavourable estimation of Bergson is most widely known from his best-selling *History of Western Philosophy*.[5] Of Russell's thirty-one chapters in this text, only the last four deal with contemporary figures: Bergson, James, Dewey, and "the philosophy of logical analysis". But while Russell felt obliged to include an entry on Bergson, he did his utmost to tarnish Bergson's reputation in the process. Aside from claiming in his opening that Bergson's philosophy "harmonized easily with the movement which culminated in Vichy", Russell equates Bergson with ants and bees (in contrast to humans) – presumably an attempt at humour, but one that demonstrates how poorly Russell read Bergson (Russell 1945: 791 and 793).[6] Perhaps of even greater consequence for his reputation was Bergson's confrontation with Einstein. In April of 1922 Bergson and Einstein locked horns at the *Société française de philosophie*. After listening to Bergson speak for half an hour about the nature of time, space and his interpretation of special relativity, Einstein dismissively replied that the time of which the philosopher speaks does not exist – there is only a psychological time that differs from the time of physicists (Canales 2015: 5). In the ensuing controversy, vigorously pursued by advocates of the two intellectual giants, Bergson was perceived by many to have lost the debate.[7]

The direct harm caused by Russell and Einstein's personal opinions of Bergson, however, should not be overplayed. Of far greater import for the future reception of Bergson were the broader directions that academia took following the zenith of Bergsonism. As Jimena Canales notes, the debate between Bergson and Einstein marks an important moment in the twentieth-century process whereby 'science', whatever is meant by that term, is partitioned from 'the rest' of academia (Canales 2015: 7). Bergson's fate is thus caught up in the more general movement by which science eclipses philosophy, which perhaps explains why Bergson is barely mentioned in the existing biographies of Einstein despite the significance of their disagreement during the 1920s (Canales 2015: 359).[8] As for the discipline of philosophy itself, it too headed in new directions after the Great War that could not accommodate a place for Bergson: on the one hand the so-called 'analytic' tradition (which presently dominates most philosophy departments), and on the other hand a tradition stemming from German existentialism, Hegelianism, and the phenomenology of Husserl and Heidegger. While the former tradition viewed Bergson to be 'anti-intellectual', proponents of the latter frequently portrayed him as a naïve psychologist out of step with the new vogue.[9] As a result, Bergson was largely considered by the next generation of philosophers to be passé – that is, when he was considered at all.[10]

While interest in Bergson today is nowhere near the levels achieved in the last years of the *Belle Époque*, it is nonetheless considerably higher than it was in the doldrums of the 1930s–80s. Part of this turnaround can be attributed to developments in the physical and biological sciences. Bergson may have been the perceived 'loser' in his confrontation with Einstein, but it was not long before Einstein himself started to be usurped by findings in the field of quantum mechanics and other scientific areas that seemed to align well with Bergson's outlook. A much-cited example is the work of Ilya Prigogine on dissipative structures and irreversibility, but many are the connections that have been drawn between Bergson and the fields of chaos theory, complexity science, non-equilibrium thermodynamics and non-linear dynamical systems.[11] In saying this, the point should not be exaggerated. Although Bergsonians are unsurprisingly attentive to the amenable relations between recent trends in science and Bergson's philosophy of change, the percentage of contemporary scientists even aware of Bergson's name would be quite small.

As it happens, the revival of interest in Bergson can be sourced back to a far more traditional, as opposed to 'cutting-edge', conduit of thought: the *agrégation* exam in the French education system. Beginning in the 1940–1 academic year, Bergson's texts were added to the *agrégation* curriculum (Bianco 2011: 861). Bergson was still alive when this decision was taken, but his early texts, written in the late nineteenth century, were now considered to be 'classics' belonging to another age, thus making him a member of the 'history of philosophy'. The appearance of these texts on the *agrégation* forced prominent French philosophers to confront Bergson again. Many of these engagements were quite favourable. As Giuseppe Bianco informs us, in Merleau-Ponty's 1948–9 classes at the *École Normale Supérieure* he "complicated Bergson's concept of intuition and the idea of a simple 'psychologism', and stressed the usefulness of Bergson in helping us to surmount the aporias of Husserl's 'ontology of the object'" (Bianco 2011: 861). In the same year Jean Hyppolite delivered a lecture course on Bergson at Strasbourg University, after which he published four articles on Bergson that brought his work into relation with Hegelian dialectics and emphasised the ontological dimension of Bergsonism (Dosse 2010: 110). Jean Wahl also taught Bergson's philosophy during this period. Wahl's estimation of Bergson was especially high: aside from dedicating his thesis to Bergson (Dosse 2010: 110), Wahl went so far as to claim that Bergson was one of "the four great philosophers" in the history of thought (the others being Socrates/Plato, Descartes and Kant) (Wahl 1962: 153). These engagements suggest that even if Bergsonism had become old-hat by the 1940s, many leading French philosophers from this period still had a good awareness of, and in some cases a healthy respect for, Bergson's work. As Hyppolite would later say: "[Bergson's] thought, whether recognized or not, dominates our era" (Hyppolite 1962: 106).

One young student during the 1940s most definitely did recognise the significance of Bergson: Gilles Deleuze. In 1948, when Deleuze was preparing for the *agrégation*, Bergson's *Matter and Memory* was one of the four texts on the programme for the Great Oral Exam. Olivier Revault d'Allonnes recalls that in a discussion with Deleuze he confessed to being irritated by Bergson. In response Deleuze said "No, you're mistaken, you've read him badly. He's a very great philosopher", after which Deleuze pulled out his copy of the text and began to extemporise (Dosse 2010: 97–8). From this anecdote we can see not only the route by which Deleuze first came to Bergson, but also how his appreciation of Bergson at this time placed him apart from the avant-garde. Deleuze describes the situation as follows:

[T]here are people these days who laugh at me simply for having written about Bergson at all. It simply shows they don't know enough history. They've no idea how much hatred Bergson managed to stir up in the French university system at the outset and how he became a focus for all sorts of crazy and unconventional people right across the social spectrum. (N 6)

Deleuze was clearly unafraid to swim against the current. In 1954 he presented a paper titled "Bergson's Conception of Difference" to the *Société des amis de Bergson* (a group to which he had been introduced by Hyppolite). It would be published in 1956 – the same year that he contributed another piece on Bergson, simply titled "Bergson, 1859–1941", for Merleau-Ponty's edited collection *Les philosophes célèbres*. In 1957 Deleuze assembled for publication a selection of Bergson's writings under the heading *Memoire et vie* (with a second edition in 1963), and in 1960 he delivered a lecture course on chapter 3 of Bergson's *Creative Evolution*. Finally, in 1966 Deleuze's monograph *Bergsonism* was published. With this book his focused study of Bergson was brought to a climax, however it should be noted that nearly all of the main points and manoeuvres contained in this text can be located in Deleuze's earlier essays. Thus while *Bergsonism* is the polished final product of Deleuze's encounter with Bergson, it would be accurate to say that Deleuze's interpretation of Bergson was effectively formed by the mid-1950s.[12]

The role of Deleuze in resurrecting enthusiasm for Bergson's work cannot be overestimated. As Bianco correctly asserts: "it is absolutely certain that Deleuze's work functioned as a kind of catalyst and provoked the revival of the texts of a thinker, who, in the wake of the criticism of phenomenology and structuralism, was treated as nothing more than a pitiful relic of antiquity" (Bianco 2011: 858). But if Deleuze is the major source for much contemporary interest in Bergson, it is not exactly due to his direct writings on Bergson. To put it one way, if Deleuze's publications on Bergson were the only texts that he ever wrote, it is doubtful that the return of Bergsonism would have had anywhere near the same degree of intensity. Indeed, when Deleuze's *Bergsonism* first appeared almost nobody took notice. By the 1980s, however, Deleuze was regarded as one of the most significant thinkers of the twentieth century.[13] What Deleuze had to say about Bergson, therefore, suddenly became much more noteworthy, providing a platform in the process for the dissemination of Bergson's thought to new audiences. And it is arguably this fact, more than anything else, that has facilitated the full-fledged return of Bergsonism.[14]

To this can be added the observation that Bergson is no minor influence on Deleuze. In recent years there has been a lot of superb scholarship excavating the numerous influences on Deleuze's thought. While useful and interesting, it should be borne in mind that practically none of these influences approach the level of Bergson. Providing a comprehensive account of how Deleuze's Bergsonism manifests in his subsequent work would require a whole book in itself, and as such is beyond the purview of the present text; but as the attentive reader of Deleuze will concur, traces of his Bergsonism can be found in almost all of Deleuze's major texts. His admiration for Bergson, moreover, does not dim with time: when asked by Didier Eribon in his later years to name some concepts created by twentieth-century philosophers, Deleuze offers six, the first three of which are Bergson's notions of duration, memory and the *élan vital* (TRM 380–1).[15]

One could pick out any number of other important references by Deleuze to Bergson in aid of reinforcing this point, but it must be stressed that such train-spotting would not fully account for the extent of Bergson's influence on Deleuze. More revealing is the fact that several of Deleuze's most significant concepts and themes can be tracked back to his engagement with Bergson, including the virtual/actual, multiplicity, difference, differentiation, individuation, problematisation, superior (transcendental) empiricism and the critique of negation. Many of these concepts and themes, it must be said, can also be located in other thinkers that Deleuze convenes with. But as the publication dates listed above demonstrate, Bergson comes first. The only major text to predate

"Bergson's Conception of Difference" is Deleuze's book on Hume, *Empiricism and Subjectivity* (1953).[16] It is also worth mentioning that this essay is first written a full eight years before the publication of *Nietzsche and Philosophy* (1962), for it dispels the not-uncommon view that Deleuze came to Bergson after Nietzsche.[17] As for the other figure commonly placed alongside Bergson and Nietzsche as one of the three great influences on Deleuze – Spinoza – this engagement once again post-dates Deleuze's obsession with Bergson; more than one esteemed commentator, furthermore, has suggested that Deleuze reads Spinoza through Bergson (see Durie 2002a and Ansell Pearson 2002: 112).[18]

Does this mean that everything Deleuze writes and thinks from 1954 onwards is reducible to his Bergsonism? Obviously not. It does however mean that claims about the influence of various thinkers on Deleuze should be checked against his Bergsonism. For example, it has been argued that Deleuze's interest in and understanding of individuation can be traced to Gilbert Simondon (see Iliadis 2013), but Simondon will not defend his *doctorat d'État* until 1958, which is several years after Deleuze's engagement with Bergson on this issue.[19] Deleuze's debt to Albert Lautman on the theme of problematic philosophy has also been remarked upon (see Bowden 2011: chapter 3), but again this connection is ancillary to the Bergsonian context in which Deleuze previously explores 'the problem'. This is not to deny that Deleuze extends and enhances his thoughts on such notions and themes through engagements with figures such as Simondon and Lautman, but it is rare to find instances where the Bergsonian frame, as understood by Deleuze, is repudiated or significantly deviated from.[20] A proper appreciation of Deleuze's Bergsonism is therefore necessary, if not *most* necessary, for an informed understanding of his work – a conclusion, one could add, that has been arrived at by both advocates and detractors of Deleuze.[21]

Having now established the import of Deleuze's encounter with Bergson for the contemporary shape of both Bergson studies and Deleuze studies, a brief overview of Deleuze's Bergsonism is in order.

DELEUZE'S BERGSONISM

As Bergsonians have frequently noted, Deleuze's Bergsonism is hardly orthodox. In many respects (though not all) it is a unique reading, an irreducible event in the reception of Bergson's work. It is therefore to be expected that Deleuze has at times been accused of perverting Bergson. The eminent Bergson scholar P. A. Y. Gunter, for example, has pointed out several ways in which Deleuze "misdescribes" Bergson using a "spirit of conceptual freedom" in order to create "what might be called a caricature of a philosophy" (Gunter 2009: 167–77).[22] This creative spirit of interpretation, to be sure, is a shared feature across Deleuze's various monographs on a single figure. As such, Deleuze's portrait of Bergson is not an exception in his oeuvre, but the rule, and maybe even that which *gives* the rule:

> But I suppose the main way I coped with it at the time was to see the history of philosophy as a sort of buggery or (it comes to the same thing) immaculate conception. I saw myself as taking an author from behind and giving him a child that would be his own offspring, yet monstrous. It was really important for it to be his own child, because the author had to actually say all I had him saying. But the child was bound to be monstrous too, because it resulted from all sorts of shifting, slipping, dislocations, and hidden emissions that I really enjoyed. I think my book on Bergson is a good example. (N 6)

As this description of Deleuze's own method of engagement illustrates, he is most willing to accept the charge of intellectual fecundity; this does not mean for one moment, though, that his portrayal of Bergson is 'wrong' or that he is an inattentive reader. Nor does it mean that Deleuze twists the words of Bergson to make him suit a pre-established agenda shared across his other texts. While this accusation could be levelled at Deleuze for some of his other books, it is important to remember that Deleuze's encounter with Bergson happens at a very early stage in his career. When Deleuze wrote "Bergson's

Conception of Difference" in 1954 it would be difficult to say that he had a developed philosophy of his own. It would thus be more reasonable to conclude that Deleuze's perversion of Bergson is undertaken for its own sake, and that this experience is formative for Deleuze's later thinking rather than the result of an already formed line of thought.

At this juncture, the title of Deleuze's book on Bergson becomes instructive: *Bergsonism*, not 'The Philosophy of Bergson' or something of that sort. Deleuze would definitely agree with Merleau-Ponty on distinguishing between Bergsonism and Bergson, but when Deleuze adopts the former as the title of his book we can be certain that his intention is not to refer to the 'collection of accepted opinions' inspired by Bergson that dominated the intellectual and cultural scene in the lead-up to the First World War. Such was no doubt the intention of Benda in his book of the same name, published in 1912. Perhaps Deleuze's book title is a play on Benda's, but I would suspect not as this would involve giving far too much credit to one commentator, even if he was Bergson's nemesis. More believable is that the title of *Bergsonism* was chosen by Deleuze for its ability to convey the driving ambition of his study: to give new life to the movement of Bergson's thought. 'Movement' is the key word here. In a 1985 text Deleuze will remark in passing that the various efforts to denounce and efface Bergson can be traced to a simple source – the desire to block movement (N 127). This assessment reprises a similar statement made by Deleuze eight years earlier:

> in him [Bergson] there is something which cannot be assimilated, which enabled him to provide a shock, to be a rallying point for all the opposition, the object of so many hatreds: and this is not so much because of the theme of duration, as of the theory and practice of becomings of all kinds, of coexistent multiplicities. (D 15)[23]

Deleuze is not the first to make an observation of this kind. In fact, the full quote of Walter Lippmann's infamous remark about Bergson actually reads: "if I were interested in keeping churches, constitutions, and customs fixed so that they would not change, I should regard Bergson as the most dangerous man in the world" (Lippmann 1912: 100–1). Deleuze is clearly attracted to this danger, and hopes to aid its proliferation. As he writes in the opening to the Afterword for the English transla-tion of *Bergsonism* (1988): "A 'return to Bergson' does not only mean renewed admiration for a great philosopher but a renewal or an extension of his project today" (B 115). From this we can see that Deleuze's aim is not to provide a 'straight' or 'correct' reading of Bergson (assuming that such is even possible), as a dutiful disciple of the master might. His allegiance, we must therefore say, is to Bergsonism and not Bergson. But this 'Berg-sonism' is not that of the *à la mode*. If Deleuze's engagement with Bergson is worthy of our attention today, it is because he brings forth an *élan* of Bergsonism – a nexus of movements and becomings – that is distinct from others and extremely gen-erative in turn. Insofar as this is the case, occasional leaps in reasoning, alterations in focus and at times even corrections of Bergson are to be expected. These instances, however, should be taken as evidence of Deleuze's devotion to Bergson's work. For as Charles Péguy has capably shown, one can be Bergso-nian whilst disagreeing with Bergson, since there is more in Bergsonism than Bergson.[24] Our challenge, as Deleuze sees it, is to explore where these movements and becomings can take us. Keith Ansell Pearson has perhaps said it best:

> What we find in Deleuze's commentaries and writings on Bergson, however, is never a mere historical retrieval of a great thinker, but an attempt to give philosophy a future. Deleuze's 'ethical' commit-ment to philosophy is, I believe, largely Bergsonian in its inspira-tion: philosophy's duty consists in showing that the future means nothing other than an opening onto new creations and inventions. (Ansell Pearson 2015: 68)

In attempting to render Bergson into a vibrant and produc-tive assemblage of coexistent becomings, Deleuze's method is by no means chosen at random – it is itself Bergsonian to the core. It is an approach that strives to consider Bergson's work as a *whole*. This is said in several respects. Starting with the mundane sense of the term, we can note that Deleuze provides a reading of Bergson's philosophy that incorporates all of his major texts together.[25] But there is also a more profound sense in which the word is used – namely, Bergson's notion of the *open* whole. Because Bergson's whole is open and not closed, it is never fully 'given' or 'giveable' and subject to change. In his first book on cinema Deleuze will explain it as follows: "if the whole is not giveable, it is because it is Open, and because its nature is to change constantly, or to give rise to something new, in short, to endure" (C1 9). Deleuze is here inspired by Bergson's evocative claim that "*Wherever anything lives, there is, open somewhere, a register in which time is being inscribed*" (CE 16). What makes something whole, therefore, is not the extent to which it is hermetic but on the contrary the manner in which it opens onto an outside – other wholes and the Whole of the universe, which is itself open and unfinished. So described, *relationality* could be said to be the critical characteristic of Bergson's open whole. By relationality, however, Deleuze specifically means *externality*:

> Relation is not a property of objects, it is always external to its terms. It is also inseparable from the open, and displays a spiritual or mental existence. Relations do not belong to objects, but to the whole, on condition that this is not confused with a closed set of objects. (C1 10)

Deleuze's Bergsonism, I would suggest, must be engaged with in this manner: as an open whole that aspires to form fruitful relations with the open whole of Bergson's thought and the various wholes that we find therein. It follows that gaining an 'understanding' of Bergsonism cannot be delivered by objectifying it as an artificially closed set. We must rather seek to gain knowledge of Bergson's thought by exploring its holistic nature in all respects – including the way in which Bergson articulates and relates various wholes, the way in which they inform one another, the way in which they give rise to the Whole of Bergsonism, and the way in which this Whole itself opens out. To cite Le Roy one more time:

> An original philosophy is not meant to be studied as a mosaic which takes to pieces, a compound which analyses, or a body which dissects. On the contrary, it is by considering it as a living act, not as a rather clever discourse, by examining the peculiar excellence of its soul rather than the formation of its body, that the inquirer will succeed in understanding it. (Le Roy 2015: 1)

Having just stressed the nature of Deleuze's Bergsonism as an irreducible and open whole, it is perhaps predictable that our task now is to dissect it. Deleuze follows convention, to some extent, in his choice of the main themes and topics of his Bergsonism: intuition, duration, memory and the *élan vital*. But as several of the chapter titles of his book reveal, in each case Deleuze will pair the key term with another that is less conventional – respectively: method, multiplicity, the virtual and differentiation. A chapter is devoted to each of these pairings, with an additional chapter (4) that serves to summarise Deleuze's findings thus far and raise/address the 'so what?' question. From these five chapters can be gleaned five essential points that Deleuze works to establish:

(1) intuition is the rigorous and problematic method of Bergsonism, with three (or five) rules;
(2) Bergson's primary notion of duration is in fact underpinned by a more fundamental theory of multiplicities;
(3) the virtual, most fully developed in Bergson's study of memory, is the key concept of his ontology;
(4) Bergsonism is both dualistic and monistic in several different and complementary ways; and
(5) the movement of life is a movement of differentiation, whereby the virtual is actualised in a creative process of divergence.

14

It is crucial to note that all five of these points are significantly interwoven. This means that a full assessment of any one requires an equivalent assessment of the others *vis-à-vis the whole that they are a part of*. This is not an easy demand to satisfy, which is no doubt why most scholars who draw on Deleuze's Bergsonism invariably engage with and utilise only one or two aspects in isolation. In a similar vein, though more unfortunately, most criticisms of Deleuze's reading that I have come across suffer from a failure to adequately appreciate the whole of his Bergsonism; in the simpler cases, the 'answer' to a supposed deficiency can often be found in a location of Deleuze's Bergsonism not considered by the detractor, while in many other cases a fuller consideration of the whole is often capable of averting the perceived confrontation.

This brings us to a final major feature of Deleuze's Bergsonism that needs mentioning here: its *progressive* nature. Again, the word 'progress' is said in a number of senses. To start with, as we have already discussed, it is Deleuze's hope that his work on Bergson will contribute to the advancement of Bergsonism, by extending it in new ways and forging new relations. But at a more technical level, the reader must bear in mind that the essential points or moments of Deleuze's Bergsonism are sequentially progressive. For example, the theory of differentiation outlined in the last chapter of his book relies upon the previously explained theory of virtual coexistence, which in turn relies upon the previously explained theory of multiplicities, all of which are underpinned by the method of intuition described in the first chapter of the book. And in the other direction, elements introduced in the earlier stages of Bergsonism will need to wait for developments further down the track before they can be fully understood, making it equally difficult for the reader to cherry-pick discrete concepts and arguments without consideration for where it is they lead and why. Deleuze's Bergsonism is thus *not* like his co-authored *A Thousand Plateaus*, which is composed of chapters that can be read in any order the reader fancies. There is only one way to read Deleuze's book on

Bergson – the old-fashioned way, from page one to the end – and it is difficult to see how Deleuze could have explicated his Bergsonism in an order other than he did. This is not to say, though, that the unfolding or unravelling of Deleuze's Bergsonism is straightforwardly chronological; aside from commencing with a chapter on method that is primarily informed by one of Bergson's last publications (the two-part introduction to *The Creative Mind*), Deleuze's reading of Bergson exhibits pronounced reflexivity, with newly emerged elements augmenting the complexion of the whole. The imagery of links being connected into a chain would thus be entirely inappropriate. Rather, Deleuze's Bergsonism must be approached and thought of in the same way that Bergson thinks of time: as an open whole that gnaws into the future, swelling as it advances and leaving on things the mark of its tooth (CE 4 and 46).

1

The Method of Intuition

INTRODUCING INTUITION AS METHOD

Duration, Memory, *Élan Vital* mark the major stages of Bergson's philosophy. This book sets out to determine, first, the relationship between these three notions and, second, the progress they involve. (B 13)

The opening paragraph of Deleuze's *Bergsonism* may be brisk, but lacking in clarity it is not. From the outset we are informed by Deleuze that he aims to explain the key concepts of Bergson's philosophy and their relation to one another. All this might seem rather straightforward, but as the words 'stages' and 'progress' in the paragraph intimate, what Deleuze intends to do is in fact quite daring and provocative: he will advance a reading of the *whole* of Bergson's philosophy – which is to say a reading that incorporates the entirety of Bergson's major books, and more profoundly, a reading that explains how the emergence of Bergson's philosophy *as an open whole* involves a *progress* from one stage to the next.

If this reading is controversial, it is first and foremost because Bergson is a problem-based thinker. Each of his books revolve around a particular problem that, although related, are distinct from one another. For example, while Bergson's first book explores the riddle of free will, this is followed by a book

17

on the nature of memory in relation to matter, after which he devotes himself to exploring the philosophy and science of biological evolution and then modern physics, followed by a book on morality and religion. Bergson no doubt deploys many of the same themes and concepts across these works, such as his infamous notion of duration, but it would nonetheless be difficult to say that Bergson made an explicit attempt throughout his career to develop a philosophical system, *à la* Kant or Hegel. At most we might say that Bergson's philosophy "desires to be a proceeding", rather than a system, since the latter "calls up the static idea of a finished building" (Le Roy 2015: 13).[1] Deleuze's aim of systematising Bergson's philosophy, to render it into an 'ism' no less, might thus seem strange if not 'un-Bergsonian'.

A further tension within Deleuze's project can be gleaned from the book's first two sentences. On the one hand, his approach to Bergson's work will be sequential, showing how an idea or problem in one book is developed or leads to others in a following book. But at the same time it is equally apparent that Deleuze's account will be informed by a whole or 'ism' that is somehow separate from the discrete states of historical fact. Deleuze's opening statement thus foreshadows a conundrum that will preoccupy much of the book: how are we to understand the genesis of a whole in relation to its internal parts and external connections? Perhaps unsurprisingly, it is in Bergson's philosophy that Deleuze will locate the necessary conceptual tools for responding to this enduring problematic.

While the project of distilling the 'ism' of Bergson's philosophy is ambitious if not suspicious, precedent for reading Bergson in this manner can actually be found in Bergson's own work. In 1934, as Bergson's career was coming to an end, he published a collection of articles and lectures that were written between 1903 and 1923 under the title *La Pensée et le Mouvant* (English translation title: *The Creative Mind*). As Bergson notes in the short preface to the book, the essays "bear mainly upon the method I believe should be recommended to the philosopher" (CM iii). For its release Bergson took the opportunity to write a two-part introduction that explains how he came to develop this recommended method. This long introduction, which takes up a third of the book, also doubles as a kind of intellectual auto-biography, revealing how Bergson was led from one problem to the next and his method for doing so. Capitalising upon this retrospective exercise, Deleuze finds in this introduction the key for unlocking the whole of Bergsonism: *intuition as method.*

Given that intuition is a central and recurrent notion in Berg-sonian philosophy, Deleuze's reliance on it for his reading of Bergson is hardly radical. What is quite striking, however, is the extent to which Deleuze formalises intuition as the endur-ing methodology of Bergson's philosophy that unites and guides his oeuvre. In his seminal essay "Introduction to Metaphysics", first published in the *Revue de métaphysique et de morale* in 1903, Bergson discusses intuition at length, occasionally refer-ring to it as his 'method'. However as he admits in a letter written in 1916, Bergson's full appreciation of intuition was actually a bit late in arriving: "The theory of intuition which you stress more than that of duration only became clear to me long afterwards."[2] This version of events is then confirmed and expanded on by Bergson in the introduction of *The Creative Mind*: "Step by step [my conclusions on the subject of duration] led me to raise intuition to the level of a philosophical method" (CM 18). Deleuze latches on to these two statements, going so far as to single out intuition from the catalogue of Bergson's other major philosophical contributions. For Deleuze, intuition is not a notion or 'stage' of Bergson's philosophy in the manner that duration, memory and the *élan vital* are. Rather, "*Intuition* is the method of Bergsonism" (B 13), and thus that which *deter-mines* the progress of Bergson's philosophy.

[W]ithout the methodological thread of intuition, the relationships between Duration, Memory and *Élan Vital* would themselves remain indeterminate from the point of view of knowledge. In all of these respects, we must bring intuition as rigorous or precise method to the forefront of our discussion. (B 14)

As it happens, this agenda for Deleuze's reading of Bergson was more or less established at least a decade before the publication of *Bergsonism*. In his essay "Bergson, 1859–1941", published in 1956, Deleuze commences by naming intuition as one of the four notions that Bergson's philosophy is associated with. The other three notions – duration, memory and the *élan vital* – are the purview of Bergson's first three major books respectively (*Time and Free Will, Matter and Memory,* and *Creative Evolution*). Deleuze is also already convinced at this early point in his career that an examination of the relationship between these three notions "can show us the development and the progress of Bergsonian philosophy" (B1 22). However, before turning to address the first of these three concepts, Deleuze claims that we must first examine the fourth unassigned term: "To begin with, I will set out to examine intuition only, not because it is the essential notion, but because it can instruct us in the nature of Bergsonian problems" (B1 22). In other words, insofar as it is true that each of Bergson's major stages are contoured by a particular problem, to understand each one, let alone their relation, we must first explore *how* Bergson approaches the handling of philosophical problems – his method of *problematising* – for it is this method that will make possible both the analysis of each problematic *and* Bergsonism as a whole.

Ascertaining the mechanics of intuition "as a true method" (B1 22) is thus the first task for Deleuze's reading of Bergson. Due to the conceptual baggage that the term 'intuition' has attracted throughout the history of philosophy, Bergson has not made this an easy undertaking. Bergson was of course well aware that his use of the word intuition could lead to some confusion, but he ultimately concludes that it remains the most appropriate word, since it designates "a mode of knowing" distinct from intelligence (CM 18). Bergson, as such, relies upon his readers to take note of how *his* notion of intuition (and intelligence for that matter) differs from conventional uses of the term. As Bergson makes clear, and Deleuze dutifully recites, intuition for him is *not* an instinct or feeling: "Not one line of what I have written could lend itself to such an interpretation" (CM 69). What, then, is Bergsonian intuition? It is a mode of knowing or *way of figuring out* that Deleuze polemically asserts is "one of the most fully developed methods in philosophy", with "strict rules, constituting that which Bergson calls 'precision' in philosophy" (B 13).

Deleuze's claim here that Bergson's method of intuition is 'fully developed' and has 'strict rules' must be taken with a grain of salt, for at no point in his work does Bergson ever write 'The rules of intuition as a method are x, y and z' (or something to that effect). Indeed, it is to Deleuze that we must give the credit for strictly formalising Bergsonian intuition as a philosophical method with clearly defined rules. Bergson does, however, go to great lengths in clarifying how his method seeks, above all, 'precision' in philosophy. As the very first sentence of *The Creative Mind* tells us: "What philosophy has lacked most of all is precision" (CM 1). By 'philosophy', it should be noted, Bergson effectively means 'metaphysics', and by the 'problem of precision' he means the lack of a method that can reliably deliver precision in metaphysics, which is to say precise knowledge about metaphysical reality. In Part I of the introduction to *The Creative Mind* there will be no discussion of 'problems' or 'problematic philosophy' – that will be the subject of Part II, which poses as its guiding problem the 'stating of problems' in philosophy. But as Bergson makes clear at the start of Part II, it is none other than his pursuit of precision in philosophy that leads to the articulation of intuition as a method for problematic philosophy. Let us then briefly look at what Bergson means by 'precision' in philosophy before turning to address the ways in which intuition secures precision as a 'problematic' methodology. Following this, we should be in a position to adequately comprehend Deleuze's 'rules' of intuition as method, which comprises his first chapter of *Bergsonism*.

PRECISION IN PHILOSOPHY

There is reality, and then there are various explanations of reality. Metaphysics by and large involves the construction of philosophical concepts and systems that aim to explain reality – or more specifically, the fundamental nature of being and the world. But in almost all cases, Bergson thinks, the metaphysics advanced is "too wide for reality" (CM 1), which is to say that it can hold as true for a world or universe that is radically different from the one *we do* occupy. For instance, many metaphysical accounts "could apply equally well to a world in which neither plants nor animals have existence, only men, and in which men would quite possibly do without eating and drinking, where they would neither sleep nor dream nor let their minds wander [. . .], and where everything might just as easily go backwards and be upside down" (CM 1). If your metaphysics can do something like this then it is questionable how much it really tells us about reality, for a metaphysical explanation should correspond to reality but not a *possible* reality or a state of affairs that admits the impossible just as readily as the real. "Let us have done", Bergson implores us, "with great systems embracing all the possible, and sometimes even the impossible!" (CM 50). And in their place, "let us demand of our theory that it embrace the real so closely that between the two no other interpretation can find room" (CM 50). Or as he puts it more fully: "The only explanation we should accept as satisfactory is one which fits tightly to its object, with no space between them, no crevice in which any other explanation might equally well be lodged; one which fits the object only and to which alone the object lends itself" (CM 1).

Bergson is of the opinion that science, or more specifically mathematics, does this especially well when applied to objects of a certain kind – static objects. But when it comes to time, Bergson argues that its proper conception "eludes mathematical treatment" (CM 2). It is in this realm of 'real time', or time as flow, that metaphysics should come into its own. According to Bergson, metaphysics dates from Zeno of Elea and his various paradoxes to do with movement and change (CM 6 and 117). The unfortunate effect of these paradoxes, however, is that they have prompted philosophers from Plato onwards "to seek the true and coherent reality in what does not change" (CM 117). The nature of time, in other words, has been sought by many metaphysicians *outside* of time. Aside from precluding its object from the outset, such an approach, Bergson points out, circumvents "what our senses and consciousness perceive", substituting in its place "a more or less artificial arrangement of concepts, a hypothetical construction" (CM 7). And as Bergson goes on to say:

> One might as well discourse on the subject of the cocoon from which the butterfly is to emerge, and claim that the fluttering, changing, living butterfly finds its *raison d'être* and fulfillment in the immutability of its shell. On the contrary, let us unfasten the cocoon, awaken the chrysalis; let us restore to movement its mobility, to change its fluidity, to time its duration. Who knows but what the 'great insoluble problems' will remain attached to the outer shell? They were not concerned with either movement or change or time, but solely with the conceptual cocoon which we mistakenly took for them or for their equivalent. Metaphysics will then become experience itself; and duration will be revealed as it really is, – unceasing creation, the uninterrupted up-surge of novelty. (CM 7)

As we can see from this passage, many metaphysical analyses fall foul of Bergson's demand for 'precision' because they study the wrong object. It may be that a cocoon is easy to analyse, due to its immobility, but such knowledge is of limited value if the aim is to understand the nature of butterflies. It follows that if one wishes to understand the nature of time, movement or change, the application of a method that freezes time and/or operates outside of time in order to extract "a system of abstract general ideas" will not suffice (CM 7). A more precise explanation is required, one that remains wedded to the object under analysis – in this case time – which in turn calls for an appropriate method that itself remains within time: intuition.

As Bergson acknowledges, the nomination of intuition as the appropriate means for remaining within time may seem peculiar, for many of the great thinkers associated with the term intuition, such as Schelling and Schopenhauer, have been of the view that intelligence works within time while intuition involves the "search for the eternal" (CM 18). But for Bergson, the converse is in fact the case: whereas the intellect is a mechanism that fixates elements in time (or removes them from time) for the purposes of analysing their relations, intuition takes the movement of time – duration – as primary: "to think intuitively is to think in duration" (CM 22). Intelligence thus starts with the immobile and then 'reconstructs' mobility, like a flip-book illustration or a reel of film. Intuition, on the other hand, starts from movement and considers immobility to be an abstraction from reality. Put differently, intelligence "concerns itself with things", which is to say the static, whereas intuition is essentially concerned with change and growth (CM 22). The great advantage of the intellect is that it is well suited to abstract manipulation and the rearrangement of existing elements within an ideal realm – an aspect of human existence that is fundamental and most certainly useful. Intuition, by contrast, involves an effort that "is arduous and cannot last", which is why the effort must be constantly renewed or begun again as time continues to flow (CM 22).

Bergson thus reverses the received positioning of intelligence and intuition. For Bergson, it is the intellect that dallies with the eternal, insofar as intellectual analysis *abstracts away* from reality and presumes an atemporal realm in which to do so, whereas intuition involves going *back into* duration and is thus the effort to get back *in touch* with real time and reality. So put, intuition aims at concrete knowledge or knowledge of the concrete, as opposed to the abstract; moreover, it seeks to reach this knowledge not *by way* of the abstract, as is customary in many metaphysics, but through sustained engagement and connection *with* the concrete, since this latter route enables a tighter fit between object and explanation (i.e. metaphysical precision).

To demonstrate this, Bergson briefly reflects on some of the great concepts in philosophy – such as Substance, Ego, Idea and Will. Such uber-concepts are notable for their tendency and ability to *totalise* reality. But as Bergson argues, if these concepts are capable of "explaining everything deductively", it is because with such concepts all has "been given beforehand, in a principle which is the concept of concepts, all the real and all the possible" (CM 19). Unity is thus produced by such concepts, but it is an artificial unity that is hypothetically posited from the outset before being (unsurprisingly) rediscovered and overlaid onto reality. In addition, such concepts are like ready-made suits off the rack, "which fit nobody because they almost fit everybody" (Le Roy 2015: 23).[3] In contrast to this tradition in metaphysics, Bergson advocates a more 'intuitive' alternative, in which explanations are made to measure according to the specifics of the thing in question:

> How much more instructive would be a truly intuitive metaphysics, which would follow the undulations of the real! True, it would not embrace in a single sweep the totality of things; but for each thing it would give an explanation which would fit it exactly, and it alone. It would not begin by defining or describing the systematic unity of the world: who knows if the world is actually one? Experience alone can say, and unity, if it exists, will appear at the end of the search as a result; it is impossible to posit it at the start as a principle. Furthermore, it will be a rich, full unity, the unity of a continuity, the unity of our reality, and not that abstract and empty unity, which has come from one supreme generalization, and which could just as well be that of any possible world whatsoever. It is true that philosophy then will demand a new effort for each new problem. No solution will be geometrically deduced from another. No important truth will be achieved by the prolongation of an already acquired truth. We shall have to give up crowding universal science potentially into one principle. (CM 19–20; see also CM 71–2)

In this passage we can begin to see how the relation of intuition with movement and time calls for a problem-based method in philosophy that requires "a new effort for each new problem".[4] By associating this problematic method with 'precision' in philosophy, Bergson is also attempting to counteract the recurring accusations that his notion/method of intuition is 'fuzzy' or lacks 'rigour'. Intuition is indeed obscure, Bergson is willing to admit, but that description depends on what one means by 'clarity' and 'obscurity'. When an idea is said to be 'clear' or 'clearly presented', it is often because the idea and/or its presentation draws on elements that are *already* 'known'. Ideas of this kind may involve a new arrangement of preexisting elements, but in such instances, "Our intelligence, finding only the old in the new, feels itself on familiar ground; it is at ease; it 'understands'" (CM 23). There is, however, an alternative kind or sense of clarity when it comes to new ideas – that of the "radically new and absolutely simple idea, which catches as it were an intuition" (CM 23). In one respect, such ideas are the opposite of clear – they are obscure and incomprehensible, inasmuch as they are properly new rather than rearrangements of the old. But while such an idea may itself be obscure, its *effect* is to dissipate obscurities, which is why it is correct to align them with clarity. Unlike the first kind of clear ideas, which are clear because they rely upon already established understandings, this second kind produces *new* understandings, which in turn shed light on their surrounds.

Intuition, as such, may be obscure, but this is to be expected given that intuition aims to produce genuinely new knowledge about new and specific problems. And when it does so, "the problems we considered insoluble will resolve themselves, or rather, be dissolved, either to disappear definitively, or to present themselves in some other way" (CM 23). The effect of this so-called obscurity is thus clarity. By contrast, intellectual ideas or ideas of the intellect invariably begin life as 'clear', since they garner their intelligibility from the preexistent and 'ready-made', but for this very reason we might also say that they contribute to confusion and obscurity when attempting to

26

comprehend new problems and the 'problem of the new': "One must therefore distinguish between the ideas which keep their light for themselves, making it penetrate immediately into their slightest recesses, and those whose radiation is exterior, illuminating a whole region of thought" (CM 23).[5]

Philosophers who analyse and explain reality through the use of 'ready-made' ideas thus have a natural advantage when it comes to fabricating the initial impression of clarity, for their ideas are couched in the preexisting and shared conventions of thought and language. But to the extent that one problem *differs* from the next and each is singular in at least one respect, Bergson contends that a 'new effort' is required for each that does not merely rely upon 'ready-made' abstractions. This shift in focus from the rearrangement of the given to the articulation of the new *on its own terms*, one could say, constitutes the essence of Bergson's problematic methodology:

> But the truth is that in philosophy and even elsewhere it is a question of *finding* the problem and consequently of *positing* it, even more than of solving it. For a speculative problem is solved as soon as it is properly stated. By that I mean that its solution exists then, although it may remain hidden and, so to speak, covered up: the only thing left to do is to *un*cover it. But stating the problem is not simply uncovering, it is inventing. Discovery, or uncovering, has to do with what already exists actually or virtually; it was therefore certain to happen sooner or later. Invention gives being to what did not exist; it might never have happened. Already in mathematics and still more in metaphysics, the effort of invention consists most often in raising the problem, in creating the terms in which it will be stated. The stating and solving of the problem are here very close to being equivalent; the truly great problems are set forth only when they are solved. (CM 36–7)

Bearing these connections in mind between the pursuit of metaphysical precision and the problematising nature of intuition, we are now in a position to set out and analyse the formalised 'rules' of intuition that Deleuze derives from his reading of Bergson.

27

THE RULES OF INTUITION

Intuition, Bergson says, consists of a "simple act" (CM 136). But as we have already seen, there are multiple aspects to this simplicity. According to Deleuze, "Bergson distinguishes essentially three distinct sorts of acts that in turn determine the rules of the method" (B 14). Similar to his broader reading of Bergsonism as a whole, Deleuze's objective throughout this discussion will be to show how the multiple aspects or meanings of intuition progressively move from one to another, giving rise to a "fundamental meaning" that is able to "rediscover the simplicity of intuition as a lived act" (B 14).

First Rule: Apply the test of true and false to problems themselves. Condemn false problems and reconcile truth and creation at the level of problems.

Deleuze begins his discussion of the 'rules' exactly where we left off our examination of precision in philosophy – namely, with the suggestion that "a speculative problem is solved as soon as it is properly stated" (CM 37). The first act of the first rule thus involves a refocusing of attention away from the uncovering of solutions through the use of ready-made ideas to the creation of problems, or more exactly problematic fields, that in turn lead to the *dissolution*, rather than 'solution', of surrounding obscurities. If we rarely do the latter, Bergson conjectures, this is due to the educational training that we receive in childhood, where "it is the school teacher who 'poses' problems [and] the pupil's task is to discover the solutions" (B 15).[6] This pedagogical practice, while quite understandable and even preferable in many instances, engenders "a kind of slavery" that is the converse of the "power to decide, to constitute problems themselves" (B 15). It is at the level of problems and their constitution, therefore, that solutions are determined as such.

In shifting the emphasis from solutions to problems, it must be stressed that this does not mean Bergson is uninterested in solutions or considers them to be unimportant. As Deleuze makes clear: "On the contrary, it is the solution that counts, but the problem always has the solution it deserves, in terms of the way in which it is stated (i.e., the conditions under which it is determined as problem), and of the means and terms at our disposal for stating it" (B 16). Most interestingly, Deleuze reinforces this point by connecting the long passage from Bergson quoted immediately above to an infamous phrase from Marx: "[Humanity] inevitably sets itself only such tasks as it is able to solve, since closer examination will always show that the problem itself arises only when the material conditions for its solution are already present or at least in the course of formation" (Marx 1993: Preface). Deleuze will elaborate this point more fully in *Difference and Repetition*, where he clarifies:

> The famous phrase of the *Contribution to the Critique of Political Economy*, 'mankind always sets itself only such tasks as it can solve', does not mean that the problems are only apparent or that they are already solved, but, on the contrary, that the economic conditions of a problem determine or give rise to the manner in which it finds a solution within the framework of the real relations of the society. [. . .] More precisely, the solution is always that which a society deserves or gives rise to as a consequence of the manner in which, given its real relations, it is able to pose the problems set within it and to it by the differential relations it incarnates. (DR 186)

Deleuze may not mention Bergson in this passage, but the debt is undeniable.[7] A further connection to Nietzsche can also be located here, as the reference to society getting what it 'deserves' suggests, for as Deleuze says on the first page of *Nietzsche and Philosophy*: "we always have the beliefs, feelings and thoughts that we deserve given our way of being or our style of life" (NP 1). Putting the point more expansively:

> We always have the truths we deserve as a function of the sense of what we conceive, of the value of what we believe. Any thinkable or thought sense is only brought into effect insofar as the forces that correspond to it in thought also take hold of something,

appropriate something, outside thought. Clearly thought cannot think by itself, any more than it can find truth by itself. The truth of a thought must be interpreted and evaluated according to the forces or power that determine it to think and to think this rather than that. (NP 104)

The publication of Deleuze's book on Nietzsche predates *Bergsonism* by four years, but if we recall that Deleuze first describes this 'problematic philosophy' in his earlier essays on Bergson (B1 22; BCD 24–5), as well as his 1960 lecture course on Bergson's *Creative Evolution* (LC 25 April 1960), then this insight about the relation between truth and the 'power that determines' (or in the terminology of *Bergsonism* the 'power to decide'/'constitutive power') is arguably Bergsonian for Deleuze before it is Nietzschean. One might also note, referring back to the 'first rule' of Bergsonism, that the method of intuition is specifically concerned with determining the *truth and falsity* of problems. In this respect, the claim here is slightly different to the Nietzschean point about truth, for what the method seeks to highlight is how a *problem* can be true/false, not a solution. As Deleuze puts it in his first essay on Bergson: "It is not by chance that, when speaking of intuition, Bergson shows us the importance, in the life of the mind, of an activity that sets up and organizes problems: there are false problems more than there are false solutions, more than there are false solutions for true problems" (B1 22). Well might we then ask, in light of this somewhat cryptic statement, how is it that a *problem* can be true or false, rather than a solution to a given problem? This leads Deleuze to propose a 'complementary rule' to the first general rule, a rule that in fact explains "Bergson's great virtue": the attempt to establish "an intrinsic determination of the false in the expression 'false problem'" (B 17).

Complementary Rule: False problems are of two sorts, 'nonexistent problems', defined as problems whose very terms contain a confusion of the 'more' and the 'less'; and 'badly stated' questions, so defined because their terms represent badly analysed composites.

In Bergson's essay "The Possible and the Real" he provides a concise and accessible discussion of 'false problems'.[8] As he remarks there: "I say that there are pseudo-problems, and that they are the agonizing problems of metaphysics. I reduce them to two. One gave rise to theories of being, the other to theories of knowledge" (CM 78). The first thing to note about this quote is that when Bergson speaks of 'pseudo-problems' he is specifically referring to the field of metaphysics – or perhaps more accurately, metaphysics and epistemology. It is therefore important to acknowledge that he does not mean to suggest that *all* problems in the entirety of philosophy can be classified under these two types, let alone problems outside of philosophy. Even within the confines of metaphysics/epistemology it is doubtful that Bergson would insist upon reducing all problems to these two (which is to say that the existence of a third sort of metaphysical/epistemological problem would not necessarily negate his argument). Bergson's more modest aim is rather to "exorcise certain phantom problems which obsess the metaphysician, that is to say, each one of us" (CM 46). There is a further technical point that needs mentioning here: the two 'phantom problems' referred to in the above quotation *both* fall under the category of 'nonexistent problems'.

Bergson provides three illustrations of 'nonexistent problems'. To begin with, he questions the validity of the enduring metaphysical question: 'why is there being, why is there something rather than nothing?' This problem, Bergson accepts, will never be solved, but in saying that, "it should have never been raised" (CM 78). As the passage proceeds: "[This problem] arises only if one posits a nothingness which supposedly precedes being" (CM 78). In Bergson's view, the idea of "nothing" is an absurdity, for at the very least it "designates the absence of what we are seeking, we desire, expect" (CM 78), and such delimitations make nothing 'something'. The situation is the same when it comes to the problem of order/disorder: "why is the universe well-ordered?" For Bergson, this is the "problem of knowledge", or more exactly, a problem that the mind fabricates, for "disorder is simply the order we are not looking for" (CM 80). So as with the issue of nothing/something, the term 'disorder' is predicated on 'order', posited by/in the mind, and the suggestion that order is "superadded to an 'absence of order' implies an absurdity" (CM 80).

Bergson's final example of 'nonexistent problems' concerns the notions of the possible and the real. It is common to presume that a possibility precedes its appearance in reality. Bergson contentiously asserts, however, that the reverse is true: "For the possible is only the real with the addition of an act of mind which throws its image back into the past, once it has been enacted" (CM 81). The suggestion that the possibility of a thing appears after the thing has been realised might seem to be manifestly mistaken, but the argument here again turns on the connection between metaphysics and epistemology – which is to say, the way in which some metaphysical problems are the product of epistemological practices. When someone says that something was possible before it was realised, the term 'possible' can refer to two things. If what is meant is "that there was no insurmountable obstacle to its realisation" (CM 83), then Bergson has no qualms with this 'negative' sense of possibility. But when the term is used in a more 'positive' sense, where a possibility or several possibilities are sketched out in thought and as such preexist their realisation "under the form of an idea" (CM 83), then this leads to the pseudo-problem of 'nonexistence' described above. Thus when Bergson says that the real precedes the possible he is not arguing for backwards causation. Nor does he mean to deny that the future can be gleaned from the present in a closed abstract system devoid of duration, such as we find in mathematics. His point is rather that the 'positive' sense of possibility, as it is commonly employed in metaphysics and everyday life, involves a trick of the mind, since its formulation presupposes rather than precedes reality: "If you close the gate you know no one will cross the road; it does not follow that you can predict who will cross when you open it" (CM 83).

In each of these examples, Bergson says, the pseudo-problem of nonexistence arises out of a confusion of the 'more' with the 'less': it would appear to be obvious that there is *less* in nothing than something, *less* in disorder than order, and *less* in the possible than the real. But Bergson argues that the converse is the case: "there is more intellectual content in the ideas of disorder and nothingness when they represent something than in those of order and existence, because they imply several orders, several existences and, in addition, a play of wit which unconsciously juggles with them" (CM 81). If it is often assumed that there is more in something than nothing, etc., it is because we have a tendency to start in the wrong place – with nothing, despite the fact that pure nothingness can only exist as an idea in the mind and is thus predicated on something, a fact of reality confirmed by experience. If one starts with nothing, or with nonbeing, then it would be obvious that a 'thing' or being is more than nothing or nonbeing. A simple glance at these words written down on paper, however, alerts us to Bergson's point: the word 'nonbeing' is based on the word 'being', it is 'being' with three letters tacked on the front, just as 'nothing' is 'thing' + 'no'. There is thus more in nonbeing than being, for the former relies on the latter, along with the idea of negation and the mind that abstractly posits it. In Deleuze's words: "In the idea of nonbeing there is in fact the idea of being, plus a logical operation of generalized negation, plus the particular psychological motive for that operation (such as when a being does not correspond to our expectation and we grasp it purely as the lack, the absence of what interests us)" (B 17).

Although Deleuze's recitation of the first sort of false problem is straightforwardly drawn from Bergson, the identification of 'badly stated questions' as the second sort requires a bit more synthetic and creative construction on the part of Deleuze. Bergson commences his discussion of pseudo-problems in "The Possible and the Real" by stating: "I believe that the great metaphysical problems are in general badly stated, that they frequently resolve themselves of their own accord when correctly stated, or else are problems formulated in terms of illusion which disappear as soon as the terms of the formula are more closely examined" (CM 77). In what follows, Bergson does not mention anything about 'composites', contra Deleuze's suggestion in his 'complementary rule'. Creativity and its expansion is rather the object of Bergson's discussion: "Reality is global and undivided growth, progressive invention, duration: it resembles a gradually expanding rubber balloon assuming at each moment unexpected forms" (CM 77). But because of the way that the intellect works, as we discussed above, human intelligence segments and freezes this expanding whole when trying to understand it. When reality is manipulated and refashioned in this manner, devoid of duration, it is then no surprise that the intellect is "able to foresee any one state of the whole: by positing a definite number of stable elements one has, predetermined, all their possible combinations" (CM 77). As Bergson thus concludes, "the failure to recognize radical novelty is the original cause of those badly stated metaphysical questions" (CM 78).[9]

Deleuze departs from this presentation somewhat by claiming that badly stated problems are "a case of badly analyzed composites that arbitrarily group things that *differ in kind*" (B 18). Deleuze is not exactly wrong in this assessment, for it is true that Bergson is trying to show us in "The Possible and the Real" how badly stated metaphysical questions arise from a confusion of duration with space. It is no accident, however, that Deleuze fleshes out this analysis by calling once again on the introduction to *The Creative Mind*. As Deleuze finds there, several of the major problems that Bergson addresses, such as the problem of liberty in his first book *Time and Free Will*, are the result of a failure to properly distinguish things that differ in kind, such as duration and space. In Bergson's words, "the problem of liberty [is] a pseudo-problem born of a confusion of duration with extension" (CM 15–16). The same confusion, he then claims, is also responsible for the mistaken belief that moods can be isolated and separated, as if they were "an intensity which is measurable"

34

(CM 16). In each case a confusion is taking place between the butterfly and its cocoon. More to the point, there is a failure to properly distinguish between the two in the first place – hence the accusation that they are examples of 'badly analysed composites'.

In "The Possible and the Real" Bergson suggests in passing that "the habit of proceeding from emptiness to fullness" (i.e. 'nonexistent problems') is already implied in "the failure to recognize radical novelty" (i.e. badly stated questions) (CM 78). As we have just seen, their common origin can be traced to the activity of the intellect and the confusions it naturally propagates. For this reason, Deleuze concludes that "In the end, there is only one kind of false problem, problems whose propositions fail to respect differences of nature" (BCD 35). The real beauty of Deleuze's reading, however, is to further link this analysis back to the demand for 'precision' in philosophy and the method of intuition that delivers it. In Part II of his introduction to *The Creative Mind*, Bergson reprises the critique of 'nonexistent problems' (see CM 46–9). After finishing this reiteration, Bergson then reminds us that the intended effect of clearing up these confusions is to bring philosophy "to a higher precision" (CM 50). Recalling our previous examination, Bergson's pursuit of precision involves a battle against 'abstract general ideas' that are divorced from concrete reality. Bergson's recommendation that we reverse the usual positioning of the 'more' and the 'less' must therefore be treated with caution, for he does not mean to suggest that we commence metaphysical inquiry by positing a vague general idea of 'some' thing. As Deleuze correctly notes, what Bergsonism actually condemns "is the obsession *in all its aspects* with thinking in terms of more and less" (B 19).

> The idea of disorder appears when, instead of seeing that there are two or more irreducible orders (for example, that of life and that of mechanism, each present when the other is absent), we retain only a general idea of order that we confine ourselves to opposing to disorder and to thinking in correlation with the idea of disorder. The idea of nonbeing appears when, instead of grasping the different realities that are indefinitely substituted for one another, we

muddle them together in the homogeneity of a Being in general, which can only be opposed to nothingness, be related to nothingness. The idea of the possible appears when, instead of grasping each existent in its novelty, the whole of existence is related to a preformed element, from which everything is supposed to emerge by simple 'realization'. (B 19–20)

This is no minor point in Deleuze's Bergsonism, and it goes back to his first published essay on Bergson from 1956.[10] In that essay Deleuze advances a preliminary and highly condensed description of Bergson's critique of false problems. There he says that problems are "badly set up" when "they make of being a generality, something immovable or undifferentiated that, in the immobile ensemble in which it is set, can only be distinguished from nothingness, from non-being" (B1 24). It follows that "The Bergsonian question is therefore not: why something rather than nothing, but: why this rather than something else?" (B1 24). Bergson's approach to metaphysics thus has no more desire to start with 'some-thing' than 'no-thing'; its modus operandi rather involves the effort to articulate *this* thing and *that* thing.

> It will come as no surprise, then, that a kind of principle of sufficient reason, as well as indiscernibles, can be found in Bergson's work. What he rejects is a distribution that locates cause or reason in the genus and the category and abandons the individual to contingency, stranding him in space. Reason must reach all the way to the individual, the genuine concept all the way to the thing, and comprehension all the way to 'this'. Bergson always asks of difference: why 'this' rather than 'that'? (BCD 36)[11]

Most crucially, by replacing the abstract and generalised contraries of 'nothing' and 'something' with the aim of specifying 'this' thing and 'that' thing, the being of a thing becomes defined *by the way it differs*. "In other words, being is difference and not the immovable or the undifferentiated, nor is it contradiction, which is merely false movement. Being is the difference itself of the thing, what Bergson often calls the *nuance*" (B1 25; see also BCD 36).

To recall our earlier discussion, Bergson argued that 'precision' in philosophy, at its best, involves the pairing of a concept with a thing and only that thing. Metaphysics is for him a kind of empiricism – what Deleuze calls a "*superior empiricism*" (B 30; see also BCD 36) – in which one aims to measure and cut out for the object "a concept appropriate to the object alone, a concept one could barely say is still a concept, since it applies only to that one thing" (CM 147).[12] However as we also went on to see, while the intellect is well suited to examining static things artificially removed from time, it is intuition that must be called upon to inquire into the concrete reality of things in duration. Intuition is thus the appropriate faculty for gaining an understanding of being, for its attention to change and growth facilitates sympathy with the difference of being. Intuition "puts us in things instead of leaving us outside" (B1 23). Thus while "the intelligence is the faculty that states problems in general [. . .] only intuition decides between the true and the false in the problems that are stated [. . .]" (B 21).

Second Rule: Struggle against illusion, rediscover the true differences in kind or articulations of the real.

As we have just seen, a failure to attend to the difference of being – or being as difference – leads to a situation where things that differ in nature are grouped together under a general concept, and as such are 'badly analysed composites'. Composites are said to be well analysed, on the other hand, when the differences in kind that make up the composite are correctly ascertained. A major part of intuition as method thus involves the articulation of 'true differences in kind', a procedure that is synonymous with articulating the nature of reality itself or 'the real'.

This term 'articulate' is said here in the most technical sense: having joints, parts or distinct areas organised into a coherent or meaningful whole. Thus when Bergson speaks, as he often does, of the natural articulations of the real, what he has in mind is an exploration and description of reality according to its distinct or 'pure' parts and their joints, as if one were following the articulations of a skeletal structure. Any empirical observation of reality, in its actuality, will only ever find composites and mixtures, which is to say that we never encounter purities in nature; but if we wish to properly understand these mixtures then it will be necessary to isolate or separate out the various components that make them up. Intuition is thus "a method of division, Platonic in inspiration" (B 22). As Deleuze puts it in his 1960 lecture course on Bergson:

> Experience, says Bergson, always presents nothing but composites [*mixtes*], not purity. It is the task of intuition to divide up the composites, to find the 'purities'. Intuition is a method of division – *i.e.* it must sift and discern the real differences in kind. Experience gives no 'purity' because, by remaining on the level of things as products, experience offers no difference in kind, only differences in degree. Only *tendencies* can differ in kind. The method of intuition specifically consists in uncovering these tendencies, these 'directions'. (LC 9 May 1960; see also B1 26 and BCD 35–6)

Note the reference to 'tendencies' at the end of this quote. Most significantly, what Bergson seeks is pure tendencies, *not* pure forms. Intuition as method may be Platonic in inspiration, but Bergson has no wish to identify pure forms to which composite reality then adheres in lesser or greater degrees. His aim is rather to distil the natural *directions of movements* in a composite – directions that exist in principle (*en droit*) if never by themselves in fact.[13] In this way, experience is always a de facto mixture and what Bergson is after are the de jure tendencies or *principles* of this experience. As the trained philosopher might recognise, this description of Bergson's project has a Kantian ring to it, but Deleuze is quick to point out their major discrepancy: what intuition as method takes us towards is not the conditions of all possible experience, but the conditions of *real* experience (B 23; see also BCD 36). Thus if intuition resembles transcendental analysis, it is more precisely a transcendental *empiricism*.[14]

How, then, does this method of division actually work? The major example that Deleuze provides is taken from chapter 1 of Bergson's *Matter and Memory*, and it has to do with the nature of perception. Bergson asks, what is it that the brain does? His response is that it "complicates the relationship between a received movement (excitation) and an executed movement (response)" (B 24). The brain, in other words, establishes an interval between a bodily call and response. Recollections may "take advantage of this interval or, strictly speaking, 'interpolate themselves', [but] on the line that we are tracing, we only have, we can only have matter and movement, movement which is more or less complicated, more or less delayed" (B 24). Now, in this interval the brain holds on to information received. Specifically, Bergson says, it retains those elements that interest the organism. It follows that what we call a perception "is not the object *plus* something, but the object *minus* something, minus everything that does not interest us" (B 25). For instance, imagine there's an eagle sitting on your shoulder and you are both looking in the exact same direction. The incoming matter that reaches your eyes and the eagle's is basically the same; but the way in which our eyes react to, manipulate or hone this excitation – the perception that we carve out from this plenitude – occurs in very different ways, with respect to the interests of the organism. Put differently, there is a "*pure* virtual perception" that is the same for both the eagle and I, and at the same time there is the "real perception" that I experience, which is different from that of the eagle. Insofar as this perception is a pared down version of the matter that physically impacts upon my brain, there is, as such, a direct line of connection between my perception, the object and matter. One can then say that: "We perceive things where they are, perception puts us at once into matter, is impersonal, and coincides with the perceived object" (B 25). So construed, the difference between perception, objects and matter is one of degree, not kind. And by noting what is rightly found on this line of objectivity, we immediately see what is not: memory, which belongs on a second line, the line of subjectivity, that differs in kind from perception-object-matter. This second line is most certainly coordinate with the first – indeed, we have already located the 'interval' in which they mix, giving rise to our experience and representation of reality – but the crucial point here is that such interpenetrations are of two separate lines that differ in kind, not degree.

To be convinced of the above argument one would need to more thoroughly examine Bergson's *Matter and Memory* (which we will turn to later in this book); Deleuze's intention in these pages is to merely illustrate how the method of intuition is a method of division that separates differences in kind according to their distinct lines of articulation. This method begins in and with experience, but by following pure lines of articulation it leads us "beyond the state of experience toward the conditions of experience" (B 27). In this respect, the method of intuition is very much concerned with the specificity of experience, but for the explicit purpose of *going beyond* the 'turn of experience' to explore that which conditions it.

> [W]hen we have placed ourselves at what we have called the turn of experience, when we have profited by the faint light which, illuminating the passage from the immediate to the useful, marks the dawn of our human experience, there still remains to be reconstituted, with the infinitely small elements which we thus perceive of the real curve, the curve itself stretching out into the darkness behind them. In this sense the task of the philosopher, as we understand it, closely resembles that of the mathematician who determines a function by starting from the differential. The final effort of philosophical research is a true work of integration. (MM 241–2)

Where, one might ask, does the procedure of intuition as method take us? Although it may at first appear that Bergson's method of intuition privileges the 'human' and 'human experience', the appeal to go *beyond* the turn of experience indicates that he rather aims to "open us up to the inhuman and superhuman (*durations* which are inferior or superior to our own), to go beyond the human condition" (B 28). Indeed, in another text Bergson refers to the "final effort" mentioned above as the "effort to go beyond the human state" (CM 163; see also CM 36). This need to go beyond the human is to be expected, given that it is entirely natural for humans to "live among badly analyzed composites" due to the activity of the human intellect (B 28). But in making this point, Deleuze stresses that Bergson's objective here is not to produce general concepts for all possible experience (in the manner of Kant); to this we could add the reminder that the unity of a concept with a thing is something that must be *arrived at* rather than presupposed. If intuition takes us towards a concept, it must be "a concept modelled on the thing itself, which only suits that thing, and which, in this sense, is no broader than what it must account for" (B 28). Such a concept is not an 'actual thing' but rather a *virtual image*. As Bergson's mathematical metaphor suggests, beginning from experience we follow the curve of a differential line around the bend and out sight, losing touch with it in actuality but gaining access to its virtual image, at which point the curve can be conceptually grasped in its entirely as a *virtual whole*. This point of intersection, where virtual lines meet each other to constitute the image of the virtual whole, "finally gives us the sufficient reason of the thing, the sufficient reason of the composite, the sufficient reason of the point of departure" (B 28–9). Intuition as method can then be summed up as consisting of two movements or moments:

> First, it denotes the moment when the lines, setting out from an uncertain common point given in experience, diverge increasingly according to the differences in kind. Then, it denotes another moment when these lines converge again to give us this time the virtual image or the distinct reason of the common point. Turn and return. Dualism is therefore only a moment, which must lead to the re-formation of a monism. (B 29)

*Complementary Rule to the Second Rule: The real is not only that which is cut out (*se découpe*) according to natural articulations or differences in kind; it is also that which intersects again (*se récoupe*) along paths converging towards the same ideal or virtual point.*

To a large extent, this second 'complementary rule' has already been explained by the concluding analysis of the 'second rule'. To understand the nature of reality we must (1) 'cut it out' according to its natural articulations or differences in kind, and (2) track these lines of divergence to their point of convergence that is the virtual image. Deleuze very briefly refers to two examples of this dual movement (B 29–30). His extremely thin exposition, however, relies on preexisting mastery of Bergsonian philosophy and is arguably not needed to establish the 'complementary rule'. Let us then turn to the third and final rule of intuition.

Third Rule: State problems and solve them in terms of time rather than of space.

And so we arrive at the 'fundamental meaning' of intuition as method – "thinking in terms of duration" (B 31). Much has of course already been said in regards to the importance of time for intuition as method: we have seen how it is *through* the study of duration that Bergson develops intuition as method; we have seen how intuition for Bergson involves going *into* duration rather than abstracting out of it in space and/or the eternal; and we have seen how false problems arise from the confusion of duration with extension and the failure to recognise radical novelty – something that intuition can perform but not the intellect, which is why intuition is the appropriate means to decide on the truth and falsity of problems. As Deleuze remarks in his first published essay on Bergson:

> [O]ne of the original things about Bergson is that in his own doctrine, he organized intuition itself as a true method, a method for eliminating false problems, for setting up problems truthfully, a

method that sets them up, then, in terms of duration. [. . .] No doubt it is duration that judges intuition, as Bergson recalls on numerous occasions, but it nonetheless remains the case that it is only intuition that can, when it has become conscious of itself as a method, seek duration in things, appeal to duration, invoke duration, precisely because it owes duration all that it is. (B1 22)

All that being said, the reader might still be wondering, *how* does one state and solve problems in terms of time rather than space? The answer to this is intimated in Deleuze's 'second rule' and its 'complementary rule'. To gain precise knowledge of the real we must rediscover true differences in kind and track their articulation. When we do this, we engage in a process of division – the dividing of a composite into its pure differences in kind, one kind from another. If duration is significant in this process, it is not merely because it guides intuition when navigating problems; more profoundly, *duration is what gives the rule of division itself*. Why? Because it is that which, by definition, *differs from itself* – indeed, according to Deleuze, "Everything Bergson has to say about [duration] comes down to this" (BCD 37).

In aid of understanding this last point let us consider Deleuze's essay "Bergson's Conception of Difference" in more detail. Recall from our previous analysis that Bergsonian metaphysics eschews the generalised ideas of 'something' and 'nothing' in favour of examining *this* thing and *that* thing. Recall also that for Bergson the aim of metaphysical inquiry should be to pair as tightly as possible an object with a concept, so that for each thing there is only one adequate explanation, and vice versa. Another way of putting this would be to say that metaphysical analysis should aim to isolate a thing by explaining how it is different from everything else. Interestingly, Deleuze refers to this process as articulating the *internal difference* of a thing: "If philosophy has a positive and direct relation to things, it is only insofar as philosophy claims to grasp the thing itself, according to what it is, in its difference from everything it is not, in other words, in its *internal difference*. [. . .] This unity of the

43

thing and the concept is internal difference, which one reaches through differences of nature" (BCD 32–3). Deleuze's use of the term 'internal' here is interesting because one might have presumed that when a thing is distinguished from other things then what has been established is the nature of its *external* difference – the difference *between* two things. There is no question that intuition, at the outset, involves the separation of things according to their differences in kind, but as Deleuze says, "the difference of nature between two things is still not the internal difference of the thing itself" (BCD 33). How then do we move from the difference of nature between two things to the internal difference of the thing itself, the latter being that which defines the nature of a thing?

We must be careful at this juncture with the term 'thing'. As we saw in the 'second rule' of intuition as method, when a composite is divided into its differences in kind, the division that occurs is between *tendencies*: "It is not things, nor the states of things, nor is it characteristics, that differ in nature; it is *tendencies*" (BCD 34). So if by 'thing' is meant an object that is the result of a productive process, then such things will always be a composite – a "blending of tendencies that differ in nature" (BCD 35). But as Deleuze admits, shifting the level of our analysis from compositional things to pure tendencies does not appear at first to advance the situation a great deal:

> Certainly, the difference of nature *between* two tendencies is an improvement over the difference of degree between things, as well as the difference of intensity between beings: and yet this difference remains external; it is still an external difference. At this point, Bergsonian intuition, to be complete, does not lack an external term which could serve as a rule; if anything, Bergsonian intuition still looks too external. (BCD 36)

Deleuze responds to this perceived impasse by examining the principal example in Bergsonian philosophy that addresses the issue: the division of duration and space. According to Bergson, the notion of abstract time in modern metaphysics is a composite of space and duration, each with their respective tendencies that differ in nature (relaxation for space and contraction for duration). However, Bergson also defines duration as that which differs from itself, for the essence of time is to continually change and become other to what it was. In this respect, duration is not merely a difference of nature in contrast to other natures; more profoundly, the *nature of duration is to differ in nature*. The upshot of this is that the division at play here is not so much between two differences of nature – this nature from that nature – but rather the separation of differences of nature from differences in degree. As Deleuze will put it in *Bergsonism*: "There is thus not a difference in kind between the two halves of the division; the qualitative difference is entirely on one side" (B 31).

We can now see how what began as a separation of differences of nature, one nature from another, culminates in a separation of that which differs in nature from that which does not. Put differently, it is no longer accurate to say that the division is between two kinds of difference, this kind and that kind; rather, on one side of the ledger resides differences in kind, while on the other is differences in degree. In this division, we have moved from an articulation of external differences to a distinction between that which differs internally and that which differs externally. Of these two differences, external and internal, it is the latter that is primary. Why? Because external difference relies upon an identification of two natures to discern their difference, thereby subordinating difference to identity, whereas internal difference relies upon nothing other than itself – or more exactly, the othering of itself – to produce differences of nature (since its nature is to differ in nature). And it is for this reason that duration is so important to the method of intuition: duration, as internal difference, is what gives the rule of differentiation, facilitating as a consequence the further articulation of difference into kind/degree and one kind from another. Thinking in time is thus not merely a requirement for the separation of differences in kind; it is the means by which we access internal difference, opening out in turn onto difference in the world.

To better explain what is happening here Deleuze calls on one of Bergson's most infamous illustrations: the dissolving lump of sugar (B 31–2; see also B1 25–6). Chapter 1 of Bergson's *Creative Evolution* begins with the assertion that "The existence of which we are most assured and which we know best is unquestionably our own" (CE 1). Referring back to his previous books, Bergson then claims that when we reflect on this existence the first thing we find is change: "I find, first of all, that I pass from state to state" (CE 1). These 'states', however, are by no means discrete homogeneities. On the contrary, every state itself undergoes continual change: "states thus defined cannot be regarded as distinct elements. They continue each other in an endless flow" (CE 3). As this endless flow suggests, states do not repeat themselves, for even when a state is said to occur again it is distinct from the first instance by virtue of it being the second iteration, and it is furthermore informed by the memory of the first. Novelty is thus guaranteed, as is unforeseeability: "For to foresee consists of projecting into the future what has been perceived in the past, or of imagining for a later time a new grouping, in a new order, of elements already perceived. But that which has never been perceived, and which is at the same time simple, is necessarily unforeseeable" (CE 6). The critical question then arises: if this assessment holds for conscious beings, can we extend the findings to existence in general? At first it would appear not, for material objects seem to present opposite characteristics: "Either [a material object] remains as it is, or else, if it changes under the influence of an external force, our idea of this change is that of a displacement of parts which themselves do not change" (CE 7–8). Material objects would also seem to lend themselves to foreseeability: "A superhuman intellect could calculate, for any moment of time, the position of any point of the system in space. And as there is nothing more in the form of the whole than the arrangement of its parts, the future forms of the system are theoretically visible in its present configuration" (CE 8). Bergson's ultimate conclusion, however, is that such initial impressions are only made possible by a disregard for duration – a disregard that results from our *intellectualisation* of matter, which removes/abstracts matter from real time. The key passage reads as follows:

> Yet succession is an undeniable fact, even in the material world. Though our reasoning on isolated systems may imply that their history, past, present, and future, might be instantaneously unfurled like a fan, this history, in point of fact, unfolds itself gradually, as if it occupied a duration like our own. If I want to mix a glass of sugar and water, I must, willy nilly, wait until the sugar melts. This little fact is big with meaning. For here the time I have to wait is not that mathematical time which would apply equally well to the entire history of the material world, even if that history were spread out instantaneously in space. It coincides with my impatience, that is to say, with a certain portion of my own duration, which I cannot protract or contract as I like. It is no longer something *thought*, it is something *lived*. (CE 7–8)

The purpose of this anecdote is to demonstrate the fundamental importance of time for assessing reality. Imagine a scenario in which we assess the nature of a sugar lump using purely spatial means. In such an exercise, Deleuze points out, "all we will ever grasp are differences in degree between that sugar and any other thing" (B 31). The dimension of time is therefore needed in order to properly see how the sugar lump differs in kind from other things. Duration, moreover, does not only reveal a difference in kind between the sugar lump and other things; as the spectacle of dissolving the sugar lump in water capably shows, over time and *in* time the sugar lump itself undergoes change – it differs "first and foremost from itself" (B 32). Also take note of the means by which the dimension of time reveals itself in this example: *by my having to wait, my impatience*. From this 'little fact', it becomes apparent that it is *through* the fact of my own duration, of which I have a privileged and reliable knowledge, that the duration of the sugar lump is made evident, allowing me in turn to assess how it differs in kind. In Deleuze's words, "my own duration, such as I live it in the impatience of waiting, for example, serves to reveal other durations that beat to other rhythms, that differ in kind from mine" (B 32). This is why duration 'gives the rule' of division, and why thinking in terms of time provides the 'fundamental meaning' of intuition as method. Finally, it explains how intuition is "the movement by which we emerge from our duration, by which we make use of our own duration to affirm and immediately to recognize the existence of other durations" (B 33) – a movement that allows one to rediscover the true differences in kind or articulations of the real (second rule of intuition) and apply the test of true and false to problems (first rule of intuition).[15]

2

Duration and Multiplicity

THE IMPORTANCE OF MULTIPLICITY

As I noted at the beginning of Chapter 1, the aim of Deleuze's book on Bergson is to determine the relationship between what he considers to be the three major stages of Bergson's philosophy – duration, memory and the *élan vital* – and also to show "the progress they involve" (B 13), from one stage to the next. Deleuze's first task, however, is to outline the method by which Bergson works, since it is this method which provides the key for unlocking the whole of Bergsonism. Upon first encountering Deleuze's explication of 'intuition as method', the reader may be slightly flummoxed, for it quickly becomes apparent that in the act of explaining aspects of Bergson's method Deleuze repeatedly draws on complex and crucial elements of Bergson's philosophy, such as his notions of duration and the virtual/actual, that have yet to be properly explained. For instance, we are told that thinking in terms of duration is the 'fundamental meaning' of intuition as method, but it will not be until later in the book that Deleuze properly addresses Bergsonian duration. So if an understanding of intuition as method is necessary in order to understand the major stages of Bergson's philosophy, the converse is also the case, producing as a result the impression in many readers that they have been dropped into the middle of a conversation far-advanced.

Deleuze is not being wilfully obtuse here. As we have already seen, the method and metaphysics of Bergson's philosophy are inextricably entwined: on the one hand, Bergson's method *emerges from* the findings of his metaphysical inquiries, while on the other hand, it is *through the application* of his method that the findings of his metaphysical inquiries can be deemed as reliably accurate, which is to say 'precise'.[1] This is why it is impossible to talk about Bergson's method without simultaneously discussing the specific metaphysical investigations to which it is applied and from which it derives. Just as the ideas of Bergson's metaphysics are not 'general', so too his method cannot be artificially isolated from the reality it seeks to understand. Hence the importance of Bergson's opening remark in the second introduction of *The Creative Mind*: "These conclusions on the subject of duration were, as it seemed to me, decisive. Step by step they led me to raise intuition to the level of a philosophical method" (CM 13). To this Deleuze adds another, more obscure, reference to a letter of Bergson's, where he says: "The theory of intuition which you stress more than that of duration only became clear to me long afterwards" (B 13).[2] Deleuze can therefore be forgiven for talking about everything 'at once' in his opening chapter of *Bergsonism*. However, having now established the parameters of intuition as method, it is nevertheless incumbent upon Deleuze (and us) to go back to the beginning, as it were, and use this methodological lesson in aid of understanding the first stage of Bergson's philosophy: duration.

The most striking thing about Deleuze's examination of duration as the first stage of Bergson's philosophy, aside from its extreme brevity, is that it in fact revolves around another concept: multiplicity. The notion of multiplicity, as we will see, is central to Deleuze's Bergsonism. As Robin Durie correctly notes: "It is the primary merit of Deleuze's Bergson interpretation to have revealed the decisive role that the concept of multiplicity plays in Bergson's thought" (Durie 2000: 153; see also Ansell Pearson 2002: 2).[3] In Deleuze's view, "Too little importance has been attached to the use of this word 'multiplicity'" (B 38). He thus sets out to rectify this lacuna in Bergson studies.[4] But why, one might wonder, is Bergson's theory of multiplicity so important for Deleuze's reading of Bergson, to the extent that it dominates his study of duration?

The answer has to do with the driving concern of Bergson to understand the nature of reality and our experience of it. Recall that the purpose of intuition as method is to provide a reliable and appropriate means of dividing up the composite of experience, for the sake of better grasping the nature of reality. Experience, we said before, is always a de facto mixture – a mixture, more exactly, of duration and space. In *Time and Free Will*, many of Bergson's most compelling and evocative illustrations focus on first-person psychological experiences, such as the experience of hearing a clock-tower toll the hour. But as Deleuze points out, while such descriptions are used by Bergson to evoke the experience of duration, as a psychological experience of reality they in fact already involve a mixture or composition of duration and space. The description of duration as a psychological experience is thus insufficient, for duration, in principle, is already a *condition* of experience (B 37), playing a star role in the effort of intuition as method to take us "beyond the state of experience toward the conditions of experience" (B 27). Duration proper, therefore, must be more than mere psychological duration, since the latter already involves an element of extension. 'Pure duration', as Bergson calls it, is defined by the manner in which it is entirely *internal*, or more specifically as we saw in the last chapter, the manner in which it *differs* internally or differs *from itself*. And it was indeed for this very reason, we went on to say, that duration *is what gives the rule of division*, since it is what makes possible the distinction between that which differs from itself and that which does not. The various determinations of internal and external differentiation, at bottom, concern the determination of *how elements relate together with a whole*. Put differently, what distinguishes the two sides of the composite are the contrasting ways in which they each form a manifold or *multiplicity*. As a result, Bergson's attempt to divide or 'decompose' the composite of real experience is underpinned by a theory of multiplicity, or more precisely, the distinction of two fundamental types of multiplicity. In Deleuze's words: "The important thing here is that the decomposition of the composite reveals to us two types of multiplicity" (B 38). The remainder of Deleuze's examination of the first stage of Bergsonism will thus largely concern itself with exploring the ramifications of Bergson's two multiplicities for understanding duration, focusing in particular on the conceptual sets of the subjective and the objective, the One and the Many, and the notion of negation. Before addressing these topics in turn, let us first take a look at how Deleuze understands the two multiplicities – a dualism, it should be noted, that will have a profound influence on Deleuze's oeuvre.

THE TWO MULTIPLICITIES

Multiplicity is by no means a marginal or hidden notion in Bergson's philosophy – after all, the second chapter of *Time and Free Will*, in which Bergson infamously examines the distinction between duration and space, is titled "The Multiplicity of Conscious States; The Idea of Duration". In this respect, Deleuze's focus on multiplicity when explicating the first stage of Bergsonism is hardly radical. What is especially noteworthy about Deleuze's reading, however, is the historical account he gives to the genesis of this notion in Bergson's thought. According to Deleuze, Bergson's theory of the two multiplicities goes back to the mathematician G. B. R. Riemann. The name Riemann does not appear in any of Bergson's major texts, but Deleuze conjectures: "It is clear that Bergson, as a philosopher, was well aware of Riemann's general problems" (B 39; see also B 117).

This 'hypothesis', as Deleuze subsequently refers to it, is based on the fact that Bergson's book *Duration and Simultaneity* debates Einstein's theory of relativity – a theory "which is directly dependent on Riemann" (B 39). We will return to this debate between Bergson and Einstein in Chapter 4; for the moment it will suffice to note that, for Deleuze, an appreciation of the significance of Bergson's theory of multiplicities relies upon an understanding of the manner in which it draws from and departs from Riemann's work on the matter.

Riemann distinguishes between two types of multiplicity: *continuous* and *discrete*. As Robin Durie explains, a multiplicity is said by Riemann to be continuous when "there exists among these ways of determination a continuous path [*stetiger Obergang*] from one to the other" (Riemann 1873: 14), otherwise the multiplicity is discrete (Durie 2004: 58). For Deleuze, of further concern is the contrary forms of measure-relations involved. Discrete multiplicities "contain the principle of their own metric", whereas continuous multiplicities "found a metrical principle in something else" (B 39). A metre, by definition, is a unit of measurement, for instance of a spatial length or musical phrase, where the length or phrase is a whole or multiplicity. A metrical principle is the principle that determines the metre of the whole or multiplicity. If the metre of a multiplicity is given by the number of elements it contains – e.g. it is defined by the fact that it contains four elements, as opposed to three or five – then that multiplicity is called 'discrete', since it can be assessed on its own terms, which is to say that the discrete elements of the multiplicity can be simply counted. When comparing magnitudes of a continuous multiplicity, however, one element will be part of another. While such a magnitude can be said to be 'more or less' than another, is it not feasible to ascertain the 'how much' (i.e. the metrical number of how much one magnitude is more or less than another). So unlike discrete multiplicities, whose elements can be counted as 'units' of a homogeneous kind according to an internally derived and contained principle, with a continuous multiplicity "we must seek the ground of its metric relations outside it, in binding forces which act upon it" (Riemann 1873: 17).

Bergson, on Deleuze's reading, alters this Riemannian setup slightly, but significantly. For Bergson, continuous multiplicities "belong essentially to the sphere of duration" (B 40). Duration, as we saw in the 'Third Rule' of intuition as method, is qualitative and has to do with differences in kind, whereas space is quantitative and has to do with differences in degree. But just because duration is qualitative this does not mean that it is indivisible or unmeasurable. Rather, it means that *when* it is divided, *it changes in kind*. As Deleuze puts it in his first published essay on Bergson: "[duration is] less that which cannot be divided than that which changes its nature by being divided" (B1 28). For instance, if you have a fruit bowl containing four pieces of fruit that are all of different types, then when the collection of fruit is divided you end up with two parts that differ in kind, not degree. While it is possible to say that both parts are of fruit, a simple taste test would confirm that the two parts differ not merely in the number (degree) of elements but their flavour (kind). One might counter that it is possible to remove a piece of fruit from the bowl without changing the flavour of those remaining, however as the appreciation of a 'still life' painting would demonstrate, it is certainly not possible to remove (or add) a piece of fruit without changing the composition of the whole. This illustrates why 'continuous' is the appropriate word to describe this type of multiplicity: as a singular whole or composition, the multiplicity is defined by the way in which it forms a *continuity between* different parts. It also explains why a continuous multiplicity is said to be *heterogeneous* as opposed to homogeneous. Etymologically, 'homogeneous' means of the *same origin* whereas 'heterogeneous' means of *different origin*. A bowl of apples is thus a homogeneous multiplicity that is composed of elements of the same kind, allowing it to be divided into discrete parts without there being a change in kind, only degree. A heterogeneous multiplicity, on the other hand, is composed of elements that differ in kind, which means that a continuity must be formed between the parts for it to be a whole. Furthermore, any division of such a heterogeneous continuity would produce a change a kind. Put the other way around, a continuous multiplicity or qualitative whole can only be divided by changing it in kind. And if a continuous multiplicity or qualitative whole changes in kind every time it is divided, then this means that the principle for its metric also changes with each division. So for Deleuze's Bergson the crucial point about continuous multiplicities is not so much that they found a metrical principle in something else. What is important about continuous multiplicities, what distinguishes them from discrete multiplicities, is that the principle of their metric, and as such the means for measuring them, changes upon division. Summing up the analysis: for Riemann the key issue has to do with the way in which a principle determines how a multiplicity is divided, in one instance from within (discrete) and another instance from without (continuous); whereas for Bergson the key difference has to do with the way in which the principle alters with division (continuous) or fails to (discrete).[5]

We can now start to make sense of Deleuze's immensely dense opening description of the two multiplicities:

> One is represented by space [. . .]: It is a multiplicity of exteriority, of simultaneity, of juxtaposition, of order, of quantitative differentiation, of *difference in degree*; it is a numerical multiplicity, *discontinuous and actual*. The other type of multiplicity appears in pure duration: it is an internal multiplicity of succession, of fusion, of organization, of heterogeneity, of qualitative discrimination, or of *difference in kind*; it is a *virtual and continuous* multiplicity that cannot be reduced to numbers. (B 38)

THE SUBJECTIVE AND THE OBJECTIVE

To elaborate on his reading of the two multiplicities, Deleuze engages in a discussion of the distinction between the subjective and the objective. This might seem like an unnecessarily convoluted way of explaining the two multiplicities, and in some respects it is, but it also happens to be the way that Bergson himself articulates his theory of multiplicities in his first book, *Time and Free Will*.

Bergson begins chapter 2 of *Time and Free Will* with the question, what is number? "Number may be defined in general as a collection of units, or, speaking more exactly, as the synthesis of the one and the many" (TFW 75). On the one hand, a number is 'one' insofar as each number is unique or singular and given a name. But on the other hand, the unity of each number "covers a multiplicity of parts which can be considered separately" (TFW 76). The intelligibility of this duality, however, is based on a hidden presupposition. Specifically, the suggestion that a number contains a collection of units depends upon the assumption that the units therein are identical with one another when counted. This is not to say that the internal units are actually identical, but simply "that we agree [. . .] to neglect their individual differences and to take into account only what they have in common" (TFW 76). In one respect, therefore, the units that comprise a number-as-multiplicity are identical, but in another respect we also know that they must be distinct from one another, lest they amalgamate together and in doing so abolish the very thing that distinguishes them. We can thus say that every number is a collection of identical yet distinct units, while also being itself a unit "in so far as it is a synthesis of the units which compose it" (TFW 80).

As Bergson shows in this analysis, people are quite capable of thinking about a number as an indivisible unit, and then thinking about the same number as composed of separate units. And when one oscillates between these two images, Bergson says, one *objectifies* the number-as-multiplicity: "How could we split it up into fractions whilst affirming its unity, if we did not regard it implicitly as an extended object, one in intuition but multiple in space? [. . .] Now, the very admission that it is possible to divide the unit into as many parts as we like, shows that we regard it as extended" (TFW 81–2). The extended divisibility of a number, Bergson thinks, illustrates the *discontinuity* of number. For example, when the number 3 is thought of as comprising three indivisible parts, "we pass abruptly from one to the other" when conceiving these parts, as would be the case if we conceived of the number 3 as being composed of six indivisible parts (each part equal to 0.5). Whichever way one decides to divide up a number-as-multiplicity, the movement, as it were, from one indivisible part to the next is 'discontinuous', with a space in between each part to prevent their merging. Number is thus discontinuous when we are building it up, though the units we utilise when doing so (i.e. whether we use three ones or six halves) are themselves each irreducible during this same process. Once 'built', however, we objectify the number, "and it then appears to be divisible to an unlimited extent" (TFW 83).

This state of affairs prompts Bergson to deploy the terms subjective and objective as follows: "we apply the term *subjective* to what seems to be completely and adequately known, and the term *objective* to what is known in such a way that a constantly increasing number of new impressions could be substituted for the idea which we actually have of it" (TFW 83–4). To illustrate what he means by this, Bergson asks us to consider the experience of an emotion or feeling. Even the most basic feeling, he points out, is extremely complex and could be said to be composed of many simple elements. When experiencing a complex feeling, it would not be accurate to say that one has a distinct and isolated perception of each of the simple elements that comprise the complex feeling. It is certainly possible to bring each one to the fore in turn, but in the very act of doing so the complex feeling being experienced changes. Therefore, at the level of the subject, we would not say that the various particular simple elements of a complex feeling have each been completely actualised in their full specificity. They are no doubt all 'there', but they are *virtually* there – real and virtual, as part of a complex whole or multiplicity with interpenetrating elements, which is to say 'continuous' yet 'heterogeneous' elements. At the level of the object, however, things are quite different. If we were to 'objectify' the complex multiplicity – i.e. consider it as an objective thing – and produce a mental image of it, then the full range of distinctions within the complexity would become visible at once, at least potentially, as if they were mapped out on paper in an exploded-view diagram. At the level of the object, therefore, it is possible to simultaneously see all of the isolated actual elements contained in a complex multiplicity, leading Bergson to claim that "this actual and not merely virtual perception of subdivisions in what is undivided is just what we call objectivity" (TFW 84). We can now see what Bergson means by his assertion that: "What properly belongs to the mind [i.e. the subjective] is the indivisible process by which it concentrates attention successively on the different parts of a given space; but the parts which have thus been isolated remain in order to join with the others, and, once the addition is made, they may be broken up in any way whatever [i.e. the objective]" (TFW 84).

Deleuze's appreciation of the situation leans quite heavily on these few pages of *Time and Free Will*. At times, Deleuze straightforwardly explicates Bergson's text. For instance, he notes that "an *object* can be divided up in an infinity of ways", and when this occurs nothing changes in the "total aspect of the object" (B 40); he also quotes and explains those passages that are unambiguously central to Bergson's argument, such as his discussion of the subjective experience of a "complex feeling" (B 42). Deleuze's reading of these pages is exceptional, however, in one key respect: the importance placed on Bergson's use of the notions virtual/actual and actualisation.

> The aforementioned passage from *Time and Free Will*, wherein Bergson distinguishes the subjective and the objective, appears to be all the more important insofar as it is the first to introduce indirectly the notion of the virtual. This notion of the virtual will come to play an increasingly important role in Bergsonian philosophy. For, as we shall see, the same author who rejects the concept of *possibility* – reserving a use for it only in relation to matter and to

closed systems, but always seeing it as the source of all kinds of false problems – is also he who develops the notion of the *virtual* to its highest degree and bases a whole philosophy of memory and life on it. (B 43)

The significance of Deleuze's reading here cannot be overstated, when one considers the immense impact that the notions of the virtual/actual and actualisation will play in not only his Bergsonism but also the remainder of Deleuze's career. When considered against the original, there is little doubt that Deleuze's interpretation is taking full advantage of the benefit of hindsight, for it would not appear from the passage of *Time and Free Will* in question that Bergson himself considered the virtual to be his preeminent notion, let alone the one upon which to base his next two major books. Nevertheless, it is hard to disagree with Deleuze when he says that the explanation of the subjective and the objective given by Bergson in this passage is peculiar. Additionally, there is no denying that inextricably tied up in this odd arrangement of the subjective and the objective are the notions of the virtual/actual and actualisation. As Deleuze remarks, one could be forgiven for "thinking it a printing error" when Bergson asserts that the subjective is what seems to be completely and adequately known, as opposed to the objective, "For is it not the objective (matter) that, being without virtuality, has a being similar to its 'appearing' and finds itself therefore adequately known? And is it not the subjective that can always be divided into two parts of another nature, which it only contained virtually?" (B 123, n.12).

Foreshadowing his examination in chapter 3 of the second stage of Bergsonism, Deleuze notes in passing that this 'theme' of virtuality will be developed more clearly in Bergson's second major book, *Matter and Memory*. But bringing our attention back to the current stage under the microscope, duration, and its guiding thematic of multiplicity, Deleuze sums up Bergson's views on objectivity as follows: "In short, 'object' and 'objective' denote not only what is divided, but what, in dividing, does not change in kind" (B 41). As for the subjective, for Deleuze it is one with duration, both of which are a multiplicity that "changes in kind in the process of dividing up" (B 42). To understand why the subjective is located on the side of time and the nonnumerical multiplicity as opposed to space and the numerical multiplicity, we need to go back to Bergson's example of a 'complex feeling'. As we saw there, a complex feeling is indivisible, with interpenetrating elements that are virtually existent. Most importantly, in the act of *actualising* each part – or in this example, concentrating attention on a particular aspect of the complex feeling – the complex feeling being experienced changes. It changes because time moves on, and because the actualisation intensifies the complex feeling in a particular way (and not others). Put otherwise, different intensities are brought to the surface, or *differentiated*, through an act of *differentiation* (a process that we will examine in more detail in Chapter 5). All of this means that the subjective dimension, as illustrated in this example, involves a *complexe* or multiplicity that is indivisible – which is to say that it changes in nature when divided, as demonstrated by the differentiation and actualisation of a particular element over time and in time.[6] The thread from Bergsonian duration to multiplicity and the subjective/objective thus becomes apparent. Duration may be the name of the first major stage of Bergsonism, but the backing theme of this analysis is provided by Bergson's theory of the two multiplicities – a thematic that is itself revealed by and applied to the distinction between the subjective and the objective.

THE ONE AND THE MANY

There are two further defining lessons that Deleuze extracts from Bergson's thoughts on duration and multiplicities. As with the discussion of the subjective and the objective, the first of these is mentioned in the opening of chapter 2 of *Time and Free Will*: the One and the Many (or 'multiple'). The distinction of the One and the Many is a mainstay of philosophy, going back to the Ancient Greeks. As a fundamental dualism, several problems and paradoxes of metaphysics, including the character of transcendence and univocity, are intercalated with the way in which the relation between the One and the Many is initially framed and understood. Bergson's intervention in this long history stems from his demand, noted in the last chapter, for 'precision' in philosophy. In the same fashion as the previously discussed conceptions of 'being' and 'non-being', Bergson argues that the notions of the One and the Many are abstract generalities devoid of precision – or at the very least, are ill-suited to delivering precision in metaphysical analyses. Such abstract generalities, on their own, are incapable of delivering concrete knowledge of the real, regardless of any mental gymnastics that metaphysicians might perform when toying with their various forms. As Deleuze puts it: "There are many theories in philosophy that combine the one and the multiple. They share the characteristic of claiming to reconstruct the real with general ideas" (B 43–4). But the question is, how can we reach any precise knowledge of reality when our investigation commences with an abstract general idea and then proceeds to simply move from one such generality to another?

Deleuze illustrates the futility of this situation by recounting Bergson's critique of the 'dialectical method' – a critique that Deleuze considers to be "amongst the finest in [Bergson's] oeuvre" (B 44). Bergson's second introduction to *The Creative Mind* is again the instructive text here. Commenting on the etymology of the word 'dialectic', Bergson notes that it contains connotations to both 'dialogue' and 'distribution': "a dialectic like Plato's was both a conversation where one sought to agree upon the meaning of the word and a distribution of things according to the indications of language" (CM 63). Metaphysics, however, runs into danger when it comes to overly rely on the conventions on language in order to arrive at knowledge of reality. As Bergson succinctly puts it in his 1911 lecture "Philosophical Intuition", "it would be a strange mistake to take for a constitutive element of doctrine what was only the means of expressing it" (CM 91). This lesson is of the

utmost importance to Bergson, and in a way serves as the starting point for his own philosophy: "My initiation into the true
philosophical method began the moment I threw overboard
verbal solutions" (CM 71). The dialectical method, according to Bergson, "attempts to construct a metaphysics with the
rudimentary knowledge one finds stored up in language" (CM
71). More specifically, it begins by establishing certain facts as
'general principles', which it then attempts to apply to things
and situations outside those facts. But as Bergson asserts in
no uncertain terms: "All my philosophical activity was a
protestation against this way of philosophizing" (CM 72)
– hence the *problematising* method of Bergsonism that we
have already outlined, which demands "for each new problem,
a completely new effort" (CM 71). It is entirely understandable, and indeed 'natural', for the human mind to "extend a
conclusion logically, to apply it to other objects without actually having enlarged the circle of its investigations" (CM 71),
but the fallacy of this method resides in the belief that such an
operation is itself productive or generative.

Deleuze singles out the dialectics of Hegelianism in particular as being incompatible with the Bergsonian approach: "We
are told that the Self is one (thesis) and it is multiple (antithesis),
then it is the unity of the multiple (synthesis)" (B 44). This process of going from one opposite to another, however, is a "false
movement" that "tells us nothing" (B 44–5). If a concept is too
broad or too general to tell us anything specific about reality,
then playing it off against its opposite hardly improves the situation: "The concrete will never be attained by combining the
inadequacy of one concept with the inadequacy of its opposite" (B 44). The alternative approach that Bergson espouses,
as it happens, also goes back to Ancient Greek philosophy.
As Deleuze points out, Plato was the first to deride those who
equate the One and the Many: "In each case he [instead] asked
how, how many, when and where" (B 44). And this is where
Bergson's intervention makes its presence fully felt. In contrast
to metaphysical approaches that attempt to articulate notions of

the One and the Many at their maximal abstraction or generality, Bergson does not accept the legitimacy of the dualism from the outset, *for there can be more than one kind of unity and more than one kind of multiple.* For instance, Bergson is willing to admit that the self is both one and multiple at the same time, but this does not mean that it is multiple in the same way as all other cases where that concept is used, nor can it be adequately reduced to a primal form: "there is in it ['our self'] a multiplicity which, it must be recognized, has nothing in common with any other" (CM 148). As this passage, which is extensively quoted by Deleuze, continues: "What really matters to philosophy is to know *what* unity, *what* multiplicity, *what* reality superior to the abstract one and the abstract multiple is the multiple unity of the person" (CM 148). The question of 'what unity' will take on increasing importance for Deleuze as his book on Bergson progresses, but for now the attention of his analysis is squarely on the issue of multiplicity. For as we have seen, the key finding from Bergson's analysis of duration in *Time and Free Will* is that duration is not merely a multiplicity, *but a certain kind of multiplicity* – namely, a *continuous* multiplicity, which is clearly "not at all the same thing as the multiple" (B 46), as that notion has been commonly understood and used. The major benefit of Bergson's theory of the two multiplicities is thus that it "saves us from thinking in terms of 'One and Multiple'" (B 43) – a manoeuvre that is most certainly a decisive moment in the history of philosophy (see also TMB).

THE EVASION OF NEGATION

A final contribution of Bergsonian thought developed through his thinking of duration-multiplicity needs mentioning at this point: Bergson's evasion of 'negation'. Deleuze devotes only minimal time and space to the topic at this stage of his analysis – one paragraph, immediately preceding his concluding summary of the chapter – but he is compelled to say something on the matter due to his implicit use of it in the discussion of the

One/Many and multiplicity. As we have just seen, Bergson takes issue with dialectical approaches that proceed by positing an abstract general idea and then 'opposing' it to its contrary. Our previous discussion focused on the difficulty if not impossibility of producing knowledge of concrete reality from the play of generalities, however there is an additional problem that Bergson has with this approach: the operation of negation itself. In Deleuze's opinion, Bergson's critique and evasion of negation is no mere side-show. On the contrary, it encapsulates all of the major aspects of Bergsonism that we have thus far examined. To better appreciate what Deleuze is getting at here, and why it is so central to his reading of Bergson, it is necessary to go back to his early essays and lectures on Bergson.

Recall the title of Deleuze's second essay published on Bergson: "Bergson's Conception of Difference". To describe this essay as dense would be an enormous understatement, however at the risk of oversimplifying things one could say that the main aim of Deleuze's essay is to demonstrate how Bergson advances a conception of difference that is distinct from the tradition of negation, best represented by the Hegelian tradition that was dominant in France at the time Deleuze was working on Bergson: "Everything comes back to Bergson's critique of the negative: his whole effort is aimed at a conception of difference without negation, a conception of difference that does not contain the negative" (BCD 42). We have already been introduced to a decent portion of the story. In aid of pairing an object and concept as tightly as possible, philosophy must "grasp the thing itself", which is to say articulate its *internal difference* (BCD 32). This notion of internal difference is immensely profound, but for the same reason is not easy to conceptually grasp. This is because difference is most commonly understood and assessed as being *between* two things – i.e. what defines a thing is the way it differs from other things. Bergson, we must remember, is more specifically concerned with articulating the difference between *tendencies* rather than things per se, but even so it is only through a consideration of duration that Bergson is able to move from external to internal difference. The reason for this, to repeat the lesson from Deleuze's third rule of intuition as method, is that the very nature of duration is to change, to differ from itself. Duration is thus not merely one kind or nature in contrast to another; it certainly is of a different nature to space, but *it is also that whose nature it is to differ in nature* – hence its privileged status. "*Difference of nature has itself become a nature*" (BCD 38). And here is the real upshot: by defining the essence of duration as alteration, Bergson has effectively generated a *substantive* notion of difference. Put otherwise, through the notion of duration Bergson has given difference a nature or essence that is defined on its own, or internally, in contrast to the common external understanding and use of the term. As Deleuze puts it:

> What differs has itself become a thing, a *substance*. Bergson's thesis could be summed up in this way: real time is alteration, and alteration is substance. Difference of nature is therefore no longer between two things or rather two tendencies; difference of nature is itself a thing, a tendency opposed to some other tendency. The decomposition of the composite does not just give us two tendencies that differ in nature; it gives us differences of nature as one of the two tendencies. And just as difference has become a substance, so movement is no longer the characteristic of something, but has itself acquired a substantial character. (BCD 38)[7]

As we can now see, the great significance of duration is that it reveals to us the substance of difference (as internal difference), and in a manner that resists the temptation to reduce difference to identity (whereby difference is placed between two identities). This substance is change, alteration. In Bergson's words, "movement and change are substantial", and "substance is movement and change" (CM 130). What this substance is most certainly not is negation, contradiction and/or alterity (not to be confused with alteration) – all of which operate at a level of externality that presupposes internal difference.

> The originality of Bergson's conception resides in showing that internal difference does not go, and is not required to go as far as contradiction, alterity, and negativity, because these three notions are in fact less profound than itself, or they are viewpoints only from the outside. The real sense of Bergson's endeavor is thinking internal difference as such, as pure internal difference, and raising difference up to the absolute. (BCD 39)

Coming back to Deleuze's brief discussion of this material in chapter 2 of *Bergsonism*, things have changed slightly from the initial 1956 formulation. Deleuze begins by stating that it is conventional to distinguish two forms of the negative: limitation and opposition. A negative notion such as disorder or nonbeing, for example, can be conceived and presented as a delimiting force on order/being or as an opposition that combines with order/being to produce the sense of both. Bergson's approach, rooted in duration and multiplicity with its emphasis on differences in kind, is clearly alien to both these forms of the negative, for the practice of separating out differences in kind does not necessarily imply a relation of opposition between the different kinds, nor does it require that one kind be presented as limiting or the limit of another: "The heart of Bergson's project is to think differences in kind independently of all forms of negation: There are differences in being and yet nothing negative" (B 46). This situation is quite evident in those cases where there are several differences in kind distinguished (and not just two). But even in the dualistic moments of Bergsonism, of which there are many, the dualisms in question are rarely if ever presented in 'negative' terms, whereby one is the opposite, contradiction or limitation of the other. And the major reason for this, in the view of Deleuze, has to do with Bergson's attentiveness to the real and concomitant distaste for abstract general concepts. If one commences by positing a general idea of order or being, it is to be expected that in aid of fleshing out this general idea it is played off of its contrary, disorder and nonbeing in general; or alternatively, it is "posited as the starting point of a deterioration that leads us to disorder in general or to nonbeing in general" (B 47). In Bergson's approach, however, the focus is on distilling the nature of *this* order/being and *that* order/being. "The true problem, then, is not that of order and disorder, but that of the differentiation of order" (LC 25 April 1960). Bergson's aversion to generalist approaches thus facilitates his evasion of negation. Furthermore, we can now see how his alternative method of separation, based on his theory of the two multiplicities and a notion of internal difference derived from his investigation of duration, simultaneously sidesteps the generalist framework of the One and the Many and its reliance on operations of negation.

> In fact, it is the category of multiplicity, with the differences in kind between two types that it involves, which enables us to condemn the mystification of a thought that operates in terms of the One and the Multiple. We see, therefore, how all the critical aspects of Bergsonian philosophy are part of a single theme: a critique of the negative of limitation, of the negative of opposition, of general ideas. (B 47)

Multiplicity, on Deleuze's reading, is thus the means by which Bergson prosecutes his various metaphysical critiques and charts an alternative way forward – an achievement that stems from and in turn envelops Bergson's investigation of duration. But seeing as duration amounts to only the first major stage of Bergson's philosophy, we should not be surprised to find that the picture of Bergsonism is far from finished. If there is an inadequacy with the portrait in its current state, it is that duration, as it appears in *Time and Free Will*, is overly psychological in its presentation and handling. To draw on an opaque phrase first mentioned by Deleuze in Chapter 1, we have yet to go "beyond the turn", which is to say "beyond our own experience" (B 27). The psychological duration of this first stage, to be sure, has pointed the way, but it is left for the next stage of Bergsonism to go through this "opening onto an ontological duration" (B 49). This shift to the ontological, however, is not merely a matter for time. While the second phase of Bergsonism will have 'memory' as it problematic framework, the key outcome of this study will be 'new foundations' for assessing *space* in a manner that is commensurate with Bergson's prior work on time.

3

Memory and the Virtual

DURATION AS MEMORY

By the end of the second chapter of his book on Bergson, Deleuze has established the significance of the two multiplicities for articulating and analysing duration – the first major stage of Bergsonism. Furthermore, duration has been aligned with the heterogeneous multiplicity and the notion of internal difference. This formulation has important ramifications for how we go about thinking of heterogeneous wholes. To illustrate, if one was to try and conceive of a heterogeneous multiplicity, there are roughly two ways of doing so: it could be done *spatially*, in which one envisions the various different elements of the multiplicity sat alongside one another, like pieces of fruit in a bowl; or it could be done *temporally*, in which one envisions the various different elements succeeding one another in time, like the consecutive notes of a melody. In the first case, the various different elements are *spatially present simultaneously*, either physically or in the mind's eye. But in the second case, the various different elements are not simultaneously present in the same way, for some of the elements in question will have passed. Thus if the various different elements are to be brought together to form a heterogeneous multiplicity, it is by virtue of *memory* that this occurs. As Bergson puts it in his essay "Introduction to Metaphysics":

Inner duration is the continuous life of a memory which prolongs the past into the present, whether the present distinctly contains the ever-growing image of the past, or whether, by its continual changing of quality, it attests rather the increasingly heavy burden dragged along behind one the older one grows. Without that survival of the past in the present there would be no duration but only instantaneity. (CM 150–1)

From this it becomes clear that a proper appreciation of Bergsonian duration, which is arguably his most influential concept, will require and lead to an extensive examination of the faculty of memory – the topic of Bergson's second major book, *Matter and Memory*, which Deleuze straightforwardly understands to be the second major stage of Bergsonism.[1]

Deleuze commences this examination of the second stage with the provocative claim that duration is "essentially" and "primarily" memory (B 51). Moreover, the two are said to be "identical" and "coextensive", but with the crucial caveat that this is "valid in principle more than in fact" (B 52). On Deleuze's reading, therefore, the "special problem of memory is: How, by what mechanism, does duration become memory in fact?" (B 52). As with the previous stage of Bergsonism, Deleuze's first port of call in pursuing this problem concerns the appraisal of subjectivity – or more specifically, the distinction of the subjective from the objective. Taking his lead from chapter 1 of *Matter and Memory*, Deleuze tracks Bergson's dissection of subjective experience into five aspects: (1) the physical sensing of need; (2) the processing of this by the brain; (3) the experience of affection (the moment of pain); (4) the insertion or embodiment of recollections; and (5) the "contraction of the experienced excitation from which quality is born" (B 53). These five aspects of subjectivity, however, *"are distributed on two very different lines of fact"* (B 52) – one line pertaining to memory and the other to matter. Of these two lines, only one is actually subjective in the proper sense of the term, the other being objective. As Deleuze points out, the first two aspects listed above "obviously belong to the objective line", while the last two are on the line of subjectivity (B 53–4).

The third or middle aspect is "more complex", as it involves the intersection of the two lines (B 53).

This discussion of memory/matter, the aspects of subjectivity, and different 'lines of fact' will likely come across as somewhat arbitrary to start with, but the analysis is brought into sharper focus through the consideration of a concrete and commonly posed set of questions: How are recollections preserved? Are they 'stored' somewhere, and if so where and how? These questions continue to inspire and plague investigations in memory studies, across the sciences and humanities. But for Bergson, such questions are borne of a false problem – a 'badly analysed composite' that fails to properly distinguish differences in kind (B 54). The implied answer to the question 'where are recollections preserved' is the brain. The brain, however, falls on the side of matter and the objective, whereas recollection pertains to the subjective (B 54). To look for recollections in the brain is therefore to look for the subjective on the objective line – a search that unsurprisingly ends in failure, for at best you will find an objective manifestation of the subjective, but never the subjective in itself. If one wants to 'find' recollections, therefore, one must start by searching on the right line.

This line, as we have seen, is the line of duration. Noting this, Bergson realises that if you want to 'find' recollections, you need look no further than duration itself: recollections do not reside in matter, they reside in duration itself. To the extent that recollections exist and are preserved, they are preserved *in duration*, as befits their kind (bearing in mind that duration may not be matter, but it is nevertheless a 'substance', as we saw last chapter). In coming to this position Deleuze once again relies heavily on Bergson's second introduction to *The Creative Mind*. There Bergson remarks that "certain consequences of my first reflection [*Time and Free Will*] were not clearly perceived and definitively accepted by me until I had reached them again along a completely different road" (CM 56). This other road is *Matter and Memory*, which takes as its problem "the reciprocal action of mind and body upon one another" (CM 56). According to his retrospective account, Bergson avoided this problem in his first book due to his overriding preoccupation with investigating the nature of freedom. Having now turned to address the problem in his second book, he adopts an approach, "faithful to [his] method", that tries to "get the problem stated in less general terms and even, if possible, to give it a concrete form, to shape it to certain facts upon which direct observation could be based" (CM 57). The mind-body problem thus reduces for Bergson to a question of the cerebral localisation of memories: how is it that the brain chooses amongst memories those that can "illuminate the action begun" and excludes others (CM 57)? By what mechanism or relation does the brain bring certain memories to consciousness whilst leaving others in the unconscious, spanning in the process the apparent chasm between body and mind? Most importantly for Bergson, when the problem is framed in this manner, the body (in the form of the brain) operates as a selection-mechanism and as such "[does] not have thinking as its function but that of hindering the thought from becoming lost in dream" (CM 57). Put differently, the brain, so construed, becomes "the organ of *attention to life*" (CM 57). But having arrived at this conclusion, a more profound realisation is made:

> [O]nly then did I become aware of the fact that inward experience in the pure state, in giving us a 'substance' whose very essence is to endure and consequently continually to prolong into the present an indestructible past, would have relieved me from seeking, and would even have forbidden me to seek, where memories are preserved. They preserve themselves [. . .] (CM 57–8)

To demonstrate what he means here, Bergson asks us to pronounce a word – for example the word 'pronounce'. When articulating the second syllable, 'nounce', it is necessary to remember the first syllable 'pro'. But in this example, *where* is the first syllable when pronouncing the second? It would seem absurd to suggest that after being pronounced it has been "immediately deposited in a drawer, cerebral or otherwise, so that consciousness may come for it a moment later" (CM 58). And what applies for these two syllables, Bergson contends, also holds for words in a sentence, and sentences in a passage, *ad infinitum*: "Now, our whole life, from the time of our first awakening to consciousness, is something like this indefinitely prolonged discourse. Its duration is substantial, indivisible insofar as it is pure duration" (CM 58). The key here has to do with the substantial and indivisible nature of duration as a heterogeneous multiplicity. As Bergson argues in *Time and Free Will* (TFW 100–5), if the notion of duration is central for understanding the nature of time, it is because it beautifully illustrates how things *endure*. Imagine that you are listening to a melody you have never heard before. As each note impresses upon your ears, it not only forms a relation with the preceding notes, but determines their function and nature within the melody as an expanding whole. On the one hand, or in one direction, it is as if each note leans over the next, awaiting and anticipating the note that will follow. Whilst in the other direction, each emerging note augments the progression, 'activating' certain parts and so forth. Thus as the melody unfolds, what you will hear at each point is much more than just an individual note. What you hear is an entire progression. In other words, the character of each emerging note in a melody is contoured in part by its interconnections or relations of 'mutual penetration' with previous notes and the melodic progression. When a new note emerges, it does not so much 'replace' the previous note as form a continuity with it. This continuity is duration. Although it is common to represent this continuity as a set of discrete moments lined up in a row, Bergson claims that in reality we do not experience time as discrete instants, but rather as an interpenetrating progression – a continuity, otherwise known as a *heterogeneous multiplicity*.

This last point is crucial. While it might be convenient to use spatial examples when envisioning the notion of heterogeneous multiplicity, for instance a fruit salad in which all the various elements are 'present' together, such examples are of minimal relevance when considering the predominant context in which the notion is utilised – duration. In the context of duration, what a heterogeneous multiplicity makes 'whole' or 'continuous' is the *interconnection between the past, the present and that which is emerging.* More precisely, it has to do with the way in which the past, present and future interpenetrate to form a substantial and indivisible duration (remembering that 'indivisible' here means 'cannot be divided without changing in kind'). In considering any durational expanse, it would then seem odd to ask 'where' the first part of the duration is as the second emerges, for they are both 'there' – together in duration, an interpenetrating *durée.* This does not mean that they both 'arrive' at the same time, nor does it mean that they are impervious to change as the duration continues to unfold. But it does mean that theories which require a relocation or transference of elements out of and back into time are inconsistent with Bergson's findings on the durational quality of time as a heterogeneous multiplicity.

THE VIRTUAL ONTOLOGY OF THE PAST

The suggestion that memory, as duration, is a heterogeneous multiplicity that renders whole an expanse of time has major implications for Bergsonism. To put it in simple terms, the suggestion would seem to mitigate if not obliterate any meaningful distinction between the present and the past. In order to address this presumed paradox let's bring things back to basics.

The present must be distinct from the past, at least conceptually if not metaphysically. Nevertheless, there must also be some kind of relation between the two. The trick to time, for Bergson, therefore has to do with understanding how the present and past are *separate yet interconnected* within the whole that is 'real time', or duration. Given that the notion of heterogeneous multiplicity was defined in the same way, its relevance here becomes quite evident: a heterogeneous multiplicity such as duration is on the one hand a whole, but on the other hand it is composed of parts, such as the past and the present, that can be distinguished from one another – i.e. it is not a homogeneity. The question then arises, what is the relation between these parts? Or more specifically, *how* do the parts differ from one another? According to Bergson, many philosophies of time understand the difference between these parts as one of degree, whereby the past and the present are elements of the same kind of substance (time) that differ from one another in degree. But for Bergson, there is a difference in kind between the past and the present, time as a whole being that which continues to differ in kind from itself. Now, if we follow Bergson on this point, we might be tempted to describe this difference in kind between the past and the present as the difference between that which exists (the present) and that which used to exist or what was (the past). Such a configuration, however, relies on a quite constrained appreciation and application of the term 'existence'. For Bergson and Deleuze, the past does indeed exist, it just doesn't exist *in the same way* as the present does.

Bergson asks us, what is the present? The present, as it is often conceived, refers to what is happening 'now'; it is the point that separates the past that it once was, from the future into which it is moving. But when we think of it this way, it would actually be more accurate to describe the present as a *becoming* – that which is being continually reformed. Due to this sense of dynamic change it is also common to think of the present as that which is active, what's going on right now, in contrast to the inactivity of the past. But even if we were to accept that the past is inactive, it nevertheless still exists, and thus it still is, in one or more senses. And what is it? If the present is becoming, in the manner described above, then it would follow that *the past is being*. To illustrate, in referring to a present moment we will have to say that it was, that it used to be but is no longer, whereas a past moment is and continues to be – once it was, it will always be. Putting the point differently: the future becomes present, the present becomes past, but the past doesn't become anything, it is and always will be, hence why it is being itself. In Bergson's words:

> But how can the past, which, by hypothesis, has ceased to be, preserve itself? Have we not here a real contradiction? – We reply that the question is just whether the past has ceased to exist or whether it has simply ceased to be useful. You define the present in an arbitrary manner as *that which is*, whereas the present is simply *what is being made*. Nothing *is* less than the present moment, if you understand by that the indivisible limit which divides the past from the future. When we think this present as going to be, it exists not yet; and when we think it as existing, it is already past. (MM 193)

We can now make sense of Deleuze's somewhat cryptic remarks about the past-as-being and the present-as-becoming, which underpins his reading of the difference in kind between matter and memory:

> We have great difficulty in understanding a survival of the past in itself because we believe that the past is no longer, that it has ceased to be. We have thus confused Being with being-present. Nevertheless, the present *is not*; rather, it is pure becoming, always outside itself. It *is* not, but it acts. Its proper element is not being but the active or the useful. The past, on the other hand, has ceased to act or to be useful. But it has not ceased to be. Useless and inactive, impassive, it IS, in the full sense of the word: It is identical with being in itself. It should not be said that it 'was', since it is the in-itself of being, and the form under which being is preserved in itself (in opposition to the present, the form under which being is consummated and places itself outside of itself). At the limit, the ordinary determinations are reversed: of the present, we must say at every instant that it 'was', and of the past, that it 'is', that it is eternally, for all time. This is the difference in kind between the past and the present. (B 55)[2]

If this all sounds a bit suspicious and counter-intuitive, it may be because the examples I have been using thus far, such as the successive notes of a melody, are overtly psychological examples. Such examples, while convenient for illustrative purposes, can be misleading, for what Bergson is attempting to articulate here is not merely the experience of recollection but more precisely the nature of *pure* recollection. To remind, in reality we are only ever confronted with mixtures and composites (e.g. of time and space, memory and perception, etc.). Bergson's initial task here is to *separate out* the pure lines of difference, so that we have a better knowledge of the composite and avoid attributing things to the wrong side and treating differences in kind as degree. The object of Bergson's analysis at this point is thus not the psychological experience of recollection, since such experience will already be at the level of mixture. Rather, what Bergson is trying to do here is articulate the conditions and parameters of pure recollection that in turn circumscribe the psychological dimension. And this is why Deleuze insists on emphasising the "extra-psychological range" of Bergson's theory of memory (B 55).

At times Bergson refers to this extra-psychological range as the 'unconscious'. This can be confusing for us moderns, given that Freud's conception of the unconscious dominates our interactions with this term. But by 'unconscious' Bergson simply means that which is not present to consciousness (such as when the term is used in the phrase 'being knocked unconscious'). In Deleuze's words, "Bergson does not use the word 'unconscious' to denote a psychological reality outside consciousness, but to denote a nonpsychological reality" (B 56). Thus the past, in its not being active, *is not psychological*. Only the present is psychological. And what is the past if it is not psychological? *It is ontological*. Pure recollection is the extra-psychological reality of being – "being as it is in itself" (B 56).

Bearing all this in mind, let us return to Bergson's line of inquiry regarding the 'where' and 'how' of memories – where are they stored, and how are they recalled. But this time let's approach the question slightly differently: what happens when we 'search' for a particular recollection? The first thing that happens, according to Bergson, is we place ourselves into the past. By this is not meant a particular time and place in history. We will get to that particular moment in due course, but first we must place ourselves into the past *in general* (i.e. into the past tense). In Bergson's words:

> Whenever we are trying to recover a recollection, to call up some period of our history, we become conscious of an act *sui generis* by which we detach ourselves from the present in order to replace ourselves, first, in the past in general, then, in a certain region of the past – a work of adjustment like the focusing of a camera. But our recollection still remains virtual; we simply prepare ourselves to receive it by adopting the appropriate attitude. (MM 133)

So at this stage of the process we do not yet have the particular recollection being sought, we have not yet grasped it. The recollection is thus entirely *virtual*, in the process of being actualised. As the above passage continues: "Little by little it comes into view like a condensing cloud; from the virtual state it passes into the actual" (MM 133–4). Because this past is the past in general, one can think of it as being like a 'giant past', an 'eternal' past, and the condition for the 'passage' of every particular present, since the present does not and cannot pass without its existence. Bergson will sometimes call it a 'gigantic' and 'immemorial' Memory. This Memory is ontological, not psychological, however as the recollection being summoned condenses or is brought to the surface it "will gradually take on a psychological existence" (B 57).

Aside from the important implications of the above discussion for our thinking on the psychological and ontological dimensions of memory, a further critical development has just occurred in Deleuze's reading of Bergson: the notion of the *virtual* has been made preeminent for appreciating the second stage of Bergsonism.[3] As most students of Deleuze will agree, the virtual is one of his most significant concepts: according to Brian Massumi, the virtual "is probably the most pivotal . . . concept in Deleuze and Guattari's philosophical vocabulary"

(Massumi 1992: 34); and in the opinion of Daniel W. Smith, "Deleuze's entire philosophy is concerned with the description of this virtual domain" (Smith 1997: 172). While this is not the time or place to discuss how Deleuze develops this notion in his latter works, the point that I would like to stress here is that the virtual, as it is initially explored by Deleuze through Bergson, is a term that primarily pertains to memory and the past. Indeed, the very reason that Deleuze latches onto it is because he is at pains to sharply distinguish the past from the present and give voice to a conception of the past on its own terms.

If this is required, it is because the notion of the past is all too often reduced to that of the present. Let's go back to the question, what is the past? One common answer is that the past is what once was, which is to say that it is what the present used to be. In this respect, the past is caught between two presents: "the old present that it once was and the actual present in relation to which it is now past" (B 58). This then leads to two mistaken conclusions: (1) we believe that the past is constituted after having been present; (2) we believe that it is reconstituted by the new incoming present, which it is now the past of. These beliefs are mistaken because by reducing the past to the present in this way we have ended up converting what is a difference in kind between the two into a difference in degree. In so doing we have in fact lost the past entirely by turning it into a mode of the present. As a result, recollection is not understood on its own terms, but as a mode of perception – the difference between them again being merely one of degree when it should be of kind – leading to what Bergson calls a 'badly analysed composite'. By reducing the past to the present and failing to treat the past on its own terms, the composite of matter and memory ceases to be a composite, becoming matter entirely. "You will never recompose the past with presents, no matter what they may be" (B 57).

If the past is commonly reduced to the present, it is perhaps because the present is conventionally understood to come *before* the past. But what if this ordering was false (in the sense of a 'false problem' discussed in Chapter 1)? Consider the passage of time, as it is often understood. There is a present, p1. This present is replaced by a new present, p2, and when this happens the previous present (p1) becomes past. How does this passage occur? How does the baton of time get passed from one to the next? p1 becomes p2 at the precise moment that p2 is born. In other words, there is a moment in time in which both p1 and p2 are contemporaneous. Now remember, in a certain way p1 and p2 are the same thing, insofar as p2 is p1 but as it once was. This means that for a moment, the present becomes past at the same time it is present. In this respect, the past is constituted at the same time that it is present – and this is its paradoxical nature.

> The past would never be constituted if it did not coexist with the present whose past it is. The past and the present do not denote two successive moments, but two elements which coexist: One is present, which does not cease to pass, and the other is the past, which does not cease to be but through which all presents pass. It is in this sense that there is a pure past, a kind of 'past in general': The past does not follow the present, but on the contrary, is presupposed by it as the pure condition without which it would not pass. (B 59)[4]

Deleuze is drawing here on Bergson's article "Memory of the Present and False Recognition", first published in 1908 and later included in the collection *Mind-Energy* (*L'Énergie spirituelle*). This essay is perhaps best known for providing an insightful account of the experience commonly referred to as *déjà vu*. Bergson's explanation of this phenomenon, however, is derived from *Matter and Memory* and effectively involves an application of key findings from that book on the relation of perception and memory. In responding to the question of how a recollection is formed, Bergson says the following:

> I hold that *the formation of a memory is never posterior to the formation of perception; it is contemporaneous with it*. Step by step, as perception is created, the memory of it is projected beside it,

as the shadow falls beside the body. But, in the normal condition, there is no consciousness of it, just as we should be unconscious of our shadow were our eyes to throw light on it each time they turn in that direction. (ME 125–6)

The suggestion that a recollection is formed at the same time as its corresponding perception may sound at first absurd, but Bergson retorts that if this is not the case and perception precedes memory, then at what precise moment will the memory begin to exist? Common sense would say that it begins, or can begin, once the perception has vanished. Psychical life, however, cannot so easily be cut up into objective states, since it is a continuous and heterogeneous as opposed to a discrete multiplicity. Perception is itself composed of successive and interpenetrating parts, and insofar as this is the case the initial conundrum persists, for where and how are the anterior elements of perception held as the successive elements arrive? Furthermore, "how, then, could the recollection arise only when everything is over? And how could memory know, at any particular moment of the operation, that everything was not over yet, that perception was still incomplete" (ME 127)? Bergson thus concludes that the recollection must be "created step by step with the perception itself" (ME 127). Put otherwise, the present "is twofold at every moment" (ME 127). In each present moment, only one of these two actually interests us – perception – since "we have no need of the memory of things whilst we hold the things themselves" (ME 128). For this reason we are prone to disregard the memory that is created in tandem with perception at the point of creation, producing in turn the illusion that perception occurs before memory, when in fact the two are co-constituted and co-emerge.

These remarks about the co-constitution of perception and recollection, it must be noted, do not contradict the previously made claim that the past is *presupposed* by the present and a condition of the present passing. For as may have become apparent by now, both memory and the past have been referred to in a number of different ways. In some cases, such as the description of how a perception and its corresponding memory are created in tandem, the memory that is being referred to is a particular memory. In other cases, however, such as the suggestion that the past must be presupposed by the present in order to pass, what is being referred to is the 'past in general' or the 'gigantic'/'immemorial' Memory. Getting clear on the different sorts of memory operational in the second stage of Bergsonism must therefore now be our immediate priority.

THE FORMS OF MEMORY

As has been noted by other commentators, Bergson is not all that consistent in his usage of the term 'memory' (Perri 2014). The first, and most important form of memory for Deleuze, is often referred to as *contraction memory*. We have already encountered this kind of memory several times. In the example of an unfolding melody, first advanced by Bergson in *Time and Free Will*, each emerging note 'leans over' the next and also 'activates' preceding aspects of the melody, *contracting together* as a result various groupings of notes. Bergson's linguistic example discussed in *The Creative Mind* makes much the same point: when pronouncing a word, a contraction occurs that brings together the syllables of a word, the words of a sentence, and so on. These examples are instructive on the nature of time and primarily concern Bergson's concept of duration. But it is equally apparent that they involve the faculty of memory, hence why Deleuze opens his examination of the second stage of Bergsonism by saying that duration is essentially memory. By this he means, in part, that memories are contractions of temporal expanses rather than discrete points. Memory in this form is thus said to consist in "contracting a number of external moments in to a single internal moment" (MM 25). Moreover, "the 'subjectivity' of sensible qualities consists above all else in a kind of contraction of the real, effected by our memory" (MM 25). Memory is thus durational and duration memorial, insofar as they share the same essential nature as contractions of heterogeneity.

The basic features of contraction memory are largely provided by and developed out of Bergson's first book *Time and Free Will*. It is important to note, however, that this form of memory is distinct from two others, which Bergson describes at length in the first section of chapter 2 of *Matter and Memory*: *habit memory* and *recollection memory*. To explain the difference between these two forms Bergson employs a simple example: the learning of a lesson. In the learning of a lesson, such as how kick a ball or conjugate a verb, the lesson is repeated multiple times. With each repetition, the lesson becomes more and more solidified until it can be said that the lesson has been learnt 'by heart'. Most significantly, the better the lesson has been learnt, the more the *particular* lessons are themselves effaced. For example, imagine that one is able to kick a ball very well. The next time they go to kick a ball, they will not do so by recalling to the mind the first time they kicked a ball, any more than they will recall to the mind the memory of the last time they did so. A learnt lesson or ingrained habit thus consists in the "decomposition and then recomposition of a whole action" (MM 89–90). The word 'action' is crucial here, for it indicates how the sensori-motor mechanics of the body are always expressed in and for action. Like with a wind-up toy, the learnt lesson or trained habit is coiled in the body, capable of being released in a system of movements when provoked. The habitual memory of motor mechanics is thus a memory of the body that translates vibrations (sensations and movements) into a reaction. As the motor-habit is set in motion by an initial impulse, the learnt lesson is reiterated, or actualised, in and by the body.[5]

But if we were to *reflect* upon this training or education of the body, we would recall the individual occasions of each repetition of the lesson; we would recollect independent memories that remain unique or singular, each "as a definite event in my history" (MM 89) – for instance the first time I kicked a ball with my father, the last time I did so with my best friend, etc. Memories of this kind *retain* that which is effaced in habit memory – namely, the details of an unrepeatable event. Each memory of this kind forms a distinct *memory-image*, and when we recall or call-up such memories we make use of what Bergson calls recollection memory. Of these two kinds of memory, habit memory and recollection memory, Bergson says that only recollection memory is memory proper. In his words: "[recollection memory] appears to be memory *par excellence*. The second [habit memory], that generally studied by psychologists, is *habit interpreted by memory* rather than memory itself" (MM 95). But this novelty of memory comes at a price, as each memory-image, inasmuch as it is unique and unrepeatable, cannot be generalised. Thus while habit memory does not so much conserve past images as *prolong* their useful effect into the present, recollection memory, at its extreme, is useless for action – it is a memory of imaging, or a memory of the imagination. As Bergson puts it: "To call up the past in the form of an image, we must be able to withdraw ourselves from the action of the moment, we must have the power to value the useless, we must have the will to dream" (MM 94). There are thus two tendencies of memory, one in which we 'lose' ourselves in memory-images, and another which bears us forwards towards action and life.

At this point in proceedings we appear to have a problem: how can memory be that which allows duration to endure and yet also be useless? Put another way, if the present is by definition that which acts while the past is that which has ceased to act, how is it that the inactive past can have an impact upon the action of the present, for would this not be an activity? To address this we need to remember that although memory-images are inactive, they still exist, they are still real, they are real as *virtual*. They may not be conscious to perception, but they are still ontological. For example, if I enter a room and close the door behind me, the corridor on the other side of the door is no longer perceived and is thus ineffective on my perception;

the corridor can be said to be '*un*conscious', insofar as it is not present to my consciousness. The virtual past is real in just this way, it may fall into obscurity, but it does not cease to exist or be any less real than would a material object disappear when it is not perceived. Just as an unperceived material object can be said to be without action on perception, so the past can be said to be inactive yet virtually real (MM 182 and 187). But if I were to open the door of the room and re-emerge into the corridor, I would presumably not be astounded by what I found, for my memory of that corridor would inform my perception of it. It is as if memories would rush before my eyes or flood towards my perception, contouring my recognition. This is precisely what memory *does*: it informs activity. The past is not activity itself, for only the present acts, but it does have an effect on the present that acts by influencing from whence perception, as it were, 'sets out'; history as an existent-unconscious *canalises* towards the future as the present perception sets out to meet it. Hence our confusion about 'doing', or what it is that the past 'does' in distinction to the present. The present is action (actual) while the past is inactive (virtual) yet informative, and while to be informative may be to have an effect on action, it is not action itself; the past does not obliterate the present, *it doubles it*.

As we saw a moment ago, to imagine we must have the will to dream. This is because a memory-image, in its singularity, cannot be generalised. But the fact is *we do* associate and correlate distinct memories with the present, practically all the time, and this is necessary for action. Specifically, we associate those features of a memory that are useful, or of most use, for an action. Moreover, according to the objectives of my action, I will actualise varying levels of specificity-generality of each memory-image. For example, my memory-image of when I stepped out into the corridor this afternoon is distinct from when I did so this morning – there were different people in the corridor, the light coming through the windows was different, etc. But when I step into the corridor when leaving the office this evening, these differences will (presumably) not disorient me; I will be able to navigate the corridor due to an effort of generalisation whereby I contract together the useful elements of each individual memory-image. If I had only been in this building once before and a long time ago, then I would require a broader or deeper level of memory-image specificity in order to successfully find my way around – I would search the deeper recesses of my memory to try and remember which corridor led where. Compare this to the level of memory-image specificity required for me to duck when a ball is thrown at my head while walking in the corridor. In this latter case, I will not require the specific memories of being in this corridor (or any corridor for that matter). I will only require enough memory of, or familiarity with, the laws of physics and the experience of being hit in the head. Depending on the action, a memory-image will thus be contracted to different degrees.

We thus come back to the characteristic of contraction, though this time it is being differently deployed. Imagine a plane or a circle, AB, which contains all of your past; this circle is like a lasso that encircles every memory or moment of your past, where each memory retains its unique singularity so that no two are alike. Now imagine another circle, which

Cone of Memory

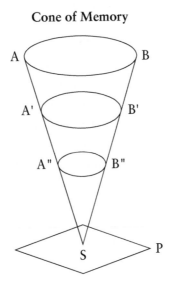

also contains the whole of your past, but in this instance each moment or memory isn't quite as detailed – so for example, all the occasions in which you kissed someone are grouped together. In this instance, the circle will contain the whole of your past, just like the other one, but the circle will be smaller, more contracted, and populated by fewer images. If you were to take all of the possible levels of contraction and stack them together in descending or ascending order, this stack would resemble a cone – Bergson's cone of memory.

As the cone of memory capably illustrates, at each present moment all of the past exists contemporaneously, and at countless degrees of contraction/*détente* (which means both expansion and relaxation in French). Most importantly, if the past or totality of memory is a cone, it is not because the larger conic sections go farther back into the past. Each section contains the entirety of the past, but at lesser or greater degrees of contraction/*détente*. In Bergson's words:

> Everything happens, then, as though our recollections were repeated an infinite number of times in these many possible reductions of our past life. They take a more common [banal] form when memory shrinks [contracts] most, more personal when it widens out [expands], and they thus enter into an unlimited number of different 'systematizations'. (MM 220; alternate translations mine)

For Deleuze, the importance of the cone of memory is of the highest order. On his reading: "This is the precise point at which contraction-Memory fits in with recollection-Memory and, in a way, *takes over from it*. Hence this consequence: Bergsonian duration is, in the final analysis, defined less by succession than by coexistence" (B 60). This is an astonishing claim to make. If Bergson's notion of duration is about anything, one would think that it is about reasserting the nature of time as succession and flow in contrast to its fixation when reduced to space. The suggestion that Bergsonian duration is defined by coexistence is therefore in hasty need of qualification.

Much of the heat can be taken out of Deleuze's claim by noting that coexistence is not instantaneity or fixation. To say that the present coexists with the past does not oblige one to hold that all of time occurs in an instant or that everything has already happened. We must also remember that the different planes of the cone are not different chronological periods of time, as if the smallest plane was the moment just gone past and the largest plane was the beginning of time. So when Deleuze says that "The whole of our past is played, restarts, repeats itself, *at the same time*, on all the levels that it sketches out" (B 61), this does not mean that time is static, devoid of movement, or that all is given in advance. Rather, it means that the whole of our past is present at any given moment, in all its varying degrees of contraction. It also means that it is necessary to have an appreciation of how the past and the present are contracted together in a duration *in order to make sense of, not deny, the indisputable fact that time continually moves or transpires.* Finally, it must be noted that the coexistence being referred to is of a *virtual* kind, not actual: "This is why the *virtual* coexistence that defines duration is at the same time a *real succession*" (BCD 47, emphasis added).

Bergson's chosen illustrations can leave us in no doubt on this point. In *Matter and Memory*, the cone of memory most certainly indicates the characteristic of coexistence, showing how the various degrees of memory-contraction coexist and relate to the plane of perception. But we must nonetheless remember that in reality the cone of memory *continuously expands in size* (a fact that can be easily forgotten if we spend too much time focusing on the spatial representation of memory-duration in a static diagram). And in his next book, *Creative Evolution*, Bergson will use the evocative example of a snowball rolling on snow to describe how memory-duration grows as it moves.

> [T]here is no feeling, no idea, no volition which is not undergoing change every moment: if a mental state ceased to vary, its dura- tion would cease to flow. Let us take the most stable of internal

states, the visual perception of a motionless external object. The object may remain the same, I may look at it from the same side, at the same angle, in the same light; nevertheless the vision I now have of it differs from that which I have just had, even if only because the one is an instant older than the other. My memory is there, which conveys something of the past into the present. My mental state, as it advances on the road of time, is continually swelling with the duration which it accumulates: it goes on increasing—rolling upon itself, as a snowball on the snow. [. . .] The truth is that we change without ceasing, and that the state itself is nothing but change. (CE 2)

The simple genius of this snowball illustration is that it perfectly expresses how memory-duration continues to move and change, but in a way that involves growth, accumulation and coexistence. As the snowball advances along the ground it expands in size, and as it moves the whole of its past moves with it. It is therefore quite right to highlight, as Deleuze does, the feature of coexistence in Bergson's theory of memory-duration, especially since this feature is absent from other well-known illustrations of time's movement (such as Heraclitus' flowing river). But it is equally clear that if contraction and coexistence are so fundamental, it is precisely in aid of explaining how time is able to pass and the unceasing nature of change, reinstating in turn the importance of succession to Bergson's notions of duration and memory.

FROM RECOLLECTION TO PERCEPTION

We do not move from the present to the past, from perception to recollection, but from the past to the present, from recollection to perception. (B 63)

Up till this point in the analysis, Deleuze's main objective has been to describe the ontological nature of memory. As we have seen, memory in principle is durational and virtual. It is also, according to Deleuze, defined primarily by contraction and coexistence, though in a manner not opposed to succession and movement but on the contrary in aid of it. Along the way we have been exposed to several forms or aspects of memory: memory in general/pure recollection, contraction memory, habit memory and recollection memory. We have also touched in passing on the relation of recollection to perception. Questions remain, however, about *how* memory, as virtual and ontological, is able to be actualised and "take on a psychological existence" (B 62). It is therefore to this end that Deleuze devotes the second half of his investigation of memory.

As discussed above, Bergson argues that the first step of this movement from the virtual to the actual involves taking a 'leap' into the past. However, when we place ourselves into the past – into the cone, as it were – we select a certain region of the past, or put differently, level of the cone. In Deleuze's words: "Depending on the case, I do not leap into the same region of the past; I do not place myself on the same level; I do not appeal to the same essential characteristics" (B 62). The way that we leap into the past in any given situation is thus influenced by "the requirements or needs of the present situation" (B 62). Put differently, the present makes an 'appeal' to the past. When it does this, the past being appealed to is no longer pure and impassive, but is rendered into "recollection-images, capable of being 'recalled'" (B 63).

Memory, Bergson says, responds to this appeal of the present with two simultaneous movements:

> one of translation, by which it moves in its entirety to meet experience, thus contracting more or less, though without dividing, with a view to action; the other of rotation upon itself, by which it turns toward the situation of the moment, presenting to it that side of itself which may prove to be the most useful. (MM 220)

These two movements – translation and rotation – are in Deleuze's view the first two aspects of memory's actualisation (B 70). Let's look at translation first. Note in the above passage how translation involves a movement of memory *in its entirety*. Note also how it involves a contraction. But what contraction, of the several that have been outlined, is being specifically referred to here? Deleuze argues that the contraction in question *is not* the contraction that produces the different levels or degrees of the cone of memory. This kind of contraction is certainly in-play, since we commenced the process by leaping into a certain region of the past – i.e. degree of contraction. But the process under examination here is the process of actualisation. When Bergson speaks of translation, therefore, he is not using this term to explain how contraction produces different virtual degrees of memory or the virtual cone at large (which is why the cone of memory can be explained without any mention of translation). It follows that the contraction being referred to in the context of translation must be of another kind: to wit, it is the contraction of a certain virtual level/degree/plane of the past with the present.

> [W]hen Bergson speaks of translation, it involves a movement that is necessary in the actualization of a recollection taken from a particular level. Here contraction no longer expresses the ontological difference between two virtual levels, but the movement by which a recollection is (psychologically) actualized, *at the same time* as the level that belongs to it. (B 64)

Two things need stressing at this point. Firstly, when a certain level of the past is contracted with the present, this does not mean that all of the intermediary levels of the cone are sandwiched together in the contraction. To reach a certain level of the cone it is not necessary to progressively pass through all the increasingly dilated degrees, which is why it is said that we 'leap' into a certain region of the past. And for the same reasons, when a virtual level of the past is actualised it is not necessary to travel back through the increasingly contracted levels. As I indicated before, the cone of memory is a useful illustration for conveying how the whole of memory and the past exists at multiple degrees of difference, but it is not intended by Bergson to represent a linear timeline (from the point to the base) or a roadmap for the route that actualisations must take (from a certain conic section passing through others consecutively towards the point). Furthermore, as Deleuze notes, the suggestion that a recollection could somehow travel up the cone through the varying levels contravenes everything that the cone stands for. If a recollection was to 'move levels' then it would no longer be that recollection; it would "lose its individuality" (B 65), and there would have been no point being on the previous level to begin with. The suggestion also fails to acknowledge that what determines the nature of a recollection on any given level *is its relation to the rest of the elements on that level.*

This brings us to the second critical point. In the act of translation, what is being contracted is not only a particular recollection with the present, *but the entire plane or level on which that recollection resides.* This needs be the case, for otherwise the isolated recollection would have no surrounding meaning or sense – i.e. what makes it a memory on 'that' level, as opposed to another. Put differently, each recollection is part of a qualitative whole or continuous multiplicity, which means that it cannot be extracted without changing it in nature. Translation therefore involves a contraction of a whole region or plane of the past with the present. But while translation is responsible for selecting the right region, another simultaneous operation or movement is needed for the recollection sought to be rendered useful: rotation.

Unlike translation, which is mentioned many times throughout *Matter and Memory*, the term rotation only appears once. The passage in which it appears, however, is of the utmost importance for understanding how recollections and the cone of memory relate to perception. Recognising its significance, Deleuze does his best to flesh out what Bergson means by rotation. Translation, as we've just seen, involves the contraction of a whole region of memory or plane of the past, not just a particular recollection on that plane, with the present perception. This plane or level of the past is not pure recollection, but neither is it a distinct recollection image. The question then is "how do we become conscious of it, how do we distinguish it in the region that is actualized with it" (B 66)? As Bergson tells us, the plane is rotated upon itself, in order to turn it towards the situation of the moment, presenting that side of itself which is of most use. So whereas translation is characterised by contraction, rotation, on Deleuze's reading, consists in the advancement of a particular aspect of the constellation. As such, rotation is defined by an *expansion* or *extension* of recollection towards perception: "it enters not only into 'coalescence', but into a kind of *circuit* with the present, the recollection-image referring back to the perception-image and vice versa" (B 66).

Translation and rotation are the first two facets of the process whereby memory takes on a psychological existence, but there are two more. These latter two involve the motor scheme and mechanics of the body. As with translation and rotation, these latter two are also kinds of movement. To explain them, Deleuze refers to two kinds of 'disturbance' that can arise in the act of recognition: (1) a *mechanical* disturbance of the motor scheme, and (2) a *dynamic* disturbance of sensori-motoricity. In the first case, recognition is inhibited because a patient no longer knows how to 'orient' herself. The recollections are no doubt there, and they can be embodied in distinct images, hence demonstrating that translation and rotation remain in operation, but "what is lacking therefore is the final moment, the final *phase*: that of action" (B 68). The recollection image, as it were, has not been made use of or rendered useful for action. In the second case, often associated with aphasia, the automatic capacity of recognition remains unimpaired, but it would seem that the recollections themselves have disappeared. But while Bergson agrees that something has indeed disappeared in instances of aphasia, he conjectures that what has been lost is not recollection itself, but "the capacity to evoke recollection, that is, to actualise it in a recollection-image" (B 69). To borrow an example mentioned by Judith Wambacq, a patient suffering from aphasia might shout "Ah, a mosquito!" when bitten by one, but then be unable to retrieve the word 'mosquito' from their memory when asked to name the flying culprit (Wambacq 2011: 313). In these cases, according to Bergson, the attitude of the body or 'corporeal attitude' is such that a *dissociation* of translation and rotation has occurred, prohibiting their insertion and combination.

> Sometimes then, translation-contraction would occur, but would lack the complementary movement of rotation, so that there would be no distinct recollection-image (or, at least, a whole category of recollection-images would seem to have been abolished). Sometimes, on the contrary, rotation would occur, distinct images would form, but they would be detached from memory and abandon their solidarity with others. (B 70)

In capping his exposition of how recollection is actualised, Deleuze says there is in fact a fifth aspect that needs mentioning. If the process of actualisation is functioning properly, then the recollection image evoked will resemble the perception image and be of use for action. In saying this, however, a recollection must be embodied not as the present it once was, but under the auspices of the new present, since time continuously moves forward, "hollowing out an interval" (B 71). The fifth aspect or movement of the process of actualisation is therefore the "*displacement* by which the past is embodied only in terms of a present that is different from that which it has been" (B 71, emphasis added).

This point brings Deleuze's analysis of the second stage of Bergsonism to a close. There is no question that the stand-out feature of Deleuze's examination, when compared to prior commentators, is his focus on the *ontological* and *virtual* dimensions of memory. But for all the limelight given to describing this "pure, virtual, impassive [and] inactive" understanding of memory, it must be acknowledged that a larger portion of the chapter on memory is spent describing "the movement of recollection in the course of actualizing itself" (B 71). So for all the emphasis placed on coexistence and contemporaneity,

94

understanding movement and change remains the driving force of Bergsonism. As Deleuze puts it in one of his earlier essays on Bergson:

> If the past coexists with itself as present, if the present is the most contracted degree of the coexistent past, then this same present, because it is the precise point at which the past is cast toward the future, is defined as that which changes nature, the always new, the eternity of life. It is understandable that a lyric theme runs through Bergson's work: a veritable hymn in praise of the new, the unforeseeable, of invention, of liberty. (B1 30–1)

It is therefore not surprising that the remainder of Deleuze's study will hone in on the implications of the first two stages of Bergsonism for complementing and correcting some prominent scientific approaches to thinking change in Bergson's day.

4

Dualism or Monism?

THE APPARENT CONTRADICTION OF BERGSONISM

There are three major stages of Bergsonism: duration, memory and the *élan vital*. In addition, there is the method, intuition, that guides the progress between these three. Deleuze dedicates a chapter to each of these four elements, but the reader will notice that there is an extra chapter in his book, placed in between his examination of the second and third stages of Bergsonism. This extra chapter is required in order to address an apparent contradiction that has emerged from the first two stages. On the one hand, Bergson's philosophy is decidedly dualistic: a great deal of effort is given to distinguishing and separating out differences in degree from differences in kind, space from time, discrete from continuous multiplicities, the objective from the subjective, matter from memory, perception from recollection, the present from the past, etc. But on the other hand, Bergsonism also exhibits a tendency towards monism. For instance, in the analysis of the relation between recollection and perception, recollections were said to *gradually* take on a psychological existence; like a condensing cloud they move from the virtual to the actual 'little by little'.[1] With descriptions like this, it would seem that the difference between them is one of degree, and that genuine differences in kind have been lost. Before continuing to the third stage of Bergsonism it is therefore necessary for

Deleuze to reconcile the dualistic and monistic dimensions of Bergson's work, to articulate their *unity* and show how Bergsonism gives rise to a "new *monism*" (B 74).

Contraction, on Deleuze's reading, is the concept that has been charged with doing the heavy lifting. As we saw in the last chapter, contraction features numerous times in Deleuze's analysis of *Matter and Memory*, and in several different ways. Contraction is what produces the cone of memory, as the different levels or planes of the cone are determined by the differing degrees to which the whole of the past is contracted. In this respect, contraction is responsible for producing the *depth* of memory, for making a *cone* of memory (rather than memory being confined to a single-solitary plane). But aside from this operation of contraction, we also saw how contraction brings together successive moments to render them contemporaneous, as part of a duration. And finally, contraction was central to the connection of recollections with perception. To this Deleuze now adds that sensation itself is a manifestation of contraction: "[Sensation] is the operation of contracting trillions of vibrations onto a receptive surface" (B 74). In this description, which suggests that quality "is nothing other than contracted quantity" (B 74), contraction is again given the pivot-role – that which brings together differences in kind. Matter thus finds its place within the schema of memory, the present within the schema of the past, as its most contracted degree. Movement and change, furthermore, are no longer alien to matter, but can be "attributed to things themselves so that material things partake directly of duration" (B 75).[2]

But can Bergson have it both ways? How is it possible to insist so strongly on the separation and irreducibility of the two sides while simultaneously claiming that there is a continuum between them that is differentiated by degrees? The notion of contraction most certainly does a good job at bringing everything together, but every step in this direction would appear to take Bergsonism towards those philosophies that reduce difference in kind to difference in degree – the very philosophies that he so strongly criticised in his first book. Moreover, any move in the opposite direction to mitigate the 'gradualist' tendency would arguably turn Bergsonism into a philosophy of abstract contrarieties and negation – another unpalatable position for Bergson. It would therefore appear that Bergsonism is in a bind of its own making. And there is one final problem thrown up by the thesis of contraction: to the extent that contraction, as illustrated by the cone of memory, distinguishes duration-memory into an infinite number of degrees, it would appear to result in a kind of 'quantitative pluralism' that precludes the emergence of any 'new monism'. The progress of Bergsonism that we have made must therefore be re-run, beginning again with duration. In so doing, Deleuze will be led by the following question: "Is duration one or many, and in what sense?" (B 76).

THE MULTIPLE AND SINGULAR NATURE OF TIME

In aid of reassessing the status of duration, Deleuze begins by drawing on Bergson's "Introduction to Metaphysics". In this essay Bergson says that there are two ways of 'knowing' something:

> The first implies going all around it, the second entering into it. The first depends on the viewpoint chosen and the symbols employed, while the second is taken from no viewpoint and rests on no symbol. Of the first kind of knowledge we shall say that it stops at the *relative*; of the second that, wherever possible, it attains the *absolute*. (CM 133)

For example, when considering the movement of an object in space, one can have a 'relative' knowledge of it, according to a particular external point of view and particular symbols to interpret and translate its movement, but if one was to inhabit the object from within then this would afford a knowledge of the object's movement that is more accurately described as absolute. To better illustrate Bergson gives concrete examples: a novelist, for instance, may describe a thousand traits of a character, but "all this has not the same value as the simple and indivisible feeling I should experience if I were to coincide for a single moment with the personage himself" (CM 134); or alternatively, "all the photographs of a city taken from all possible points of view [. . .] will never equal in value that dimensional object, the city along whose streets one walks" (CM 134).[3] Whereas relative knowledge is ascertained by intellectual analysis, the absolute, Bergson says, can only be accessed via intuition. We are thus brought back to the beginning of Bergsonism, intuition as method, and its distinction from intellectual analysis.

While it may be difficult (or more accurately impossible) for me to coincide, even for a single moment, with the character described by the novelist, "there is at least one reality which we all seize from within, by intuition and not by simple analysis. It is our own person in its flowing through time, the self which endures" (CM 136). When engaged in conscious self-reflection, I can and often will articulate all the various perceptions that I receive from the material world and recollections that I 'call up' from my memory – elements that are well-defined, "clear-cut, distinct, juxtaposed or mutually juxtaposable" (CM 136). However, these 'crystals', as Bergson terms them, are not identical to reality: beneath them, there is "a continuity of flow comparable to no other" (CM 137). We could call this flow a succession of states, but only retrospectively and 'out of time':

> While I was experiencing them they were so solidly organized, so profoundly animated with a common life, that I could never have said where any one of them finished or the next one began. In reality, none of them do begin or end; they all dovetail into one another. (CM 137)

Note how in each of the above illustrations a distinction is being made between knowledge derived from the accumulation of *multiple* states and knowledge gained from installation in a *singular* movement or flow. As this shows us, one of the key distinctions between these two ways of knowing has to do

100

with whether time is treated and understood as multiple (composed of many points) or singular (an indivisible expanse). The nature of duration as an indivisible singularity, to be sure, is itself a multiplicity – a *heterogeneous* multiplicity, as we outlined in Chapter 2. But even with this qualification, one could be forgiven for thinking that the intuitive account of duration comes across as overly individualistic, if not solipsistic, as if the nature of time itself relied upon or was reducible to my personal psychological impression of it. Bergson is well aware of this potential impression of his theory and assures us that it is not his intention to "shut the philosopher up in exclusive self-contemplation" (CM 155). Indeed, he asserts that his whole aim has been, if anything, "to affirm the existence of objects both inferior and superior to us" – or in other words, "to make them co-existent without difficulty" (CM 155).

What follows is an explanation of how intuition "is not a single act but an indefinite series of acts" that "corresponds to the degrees of being" (CM 155). Recall how Bergson's method of intuition distances itself from those dialectical approaches that commence by positing abstract generalities, such as being and nothingness 'in general', or the abstract conceptions of order and disorder. His claim was that such abstractions are a poor fit with reality and incapable of delivering 'precise' and 'concrete' knowledge of reality. We then saw in Chapter 2 how the contrary notions of the One and the Many are faulty in the same way. To this list we can now add multiplicity and unity, for "This combination can present neither a diversity of degrees nor a variety of forms: it is or it is not" (CM 155). According to the approach of positing general contrarieties, guided by intellectual analysis, the notion of duration is meant to somehow effectuate a 'synthesis' between the oppositional abstractions of multiplicity and unity. Duration, from the perspective of intellectual analysis, is thus singular: there can only be one duration, the duration that synthesises multiplicity and unity. But how, on this schema, is the movement of time explained? And where is movement located? It can't reside in the multiple moments or instants, since the very thing we are seeking to explain is the transitions between them. Equally unsatisfactory, however, is the suggestion that the movement of time is generated by the thread on which the beads are said to hang, for this abstract unity "cannot have duration either since, by hypothesis, everything that is changing and really durable in duration has been put to the account of the multiplicity of moments" (CM 156). As the inverse of multiplicity, whose essence boils down to the instant, this unity is more accurately eternity – immobile and intemporal.

But on Bergson's approach, guided by the method of intuition, things proceed rather differently. By installing oneself *in* duration, instead of externally analysing it, one has a certain sense of it; with this comes the impression that it could be sensed otherwise, whether by ourselves or other beings; and from this one perceives that there could be an infinity of other durations. In this way, our own empirical experience with duration does not preclude the existence of others, but on the contrary is the thing that confirms the existence of other durations, "all very different from one another" (CM 156). As Bergson concludes:

> [S]o the intuition of our duration, far from leaving us suspended in the void as pure analysis would do, puts us in contact with a whole continuity of durations which we should try to follow either downwardly or upwardly: in both cases we can dilate ourselves indefinitely by a more and more vigorous effort, in both cases transcend ourselves. In the first case, we advance toward a duration more and more scattered, whose palpitations, more rapid than ours, dividing our simple sensation, dilute its quality into quantity: at the limit would be the pure homogeneous, the pure *repetition* by which we shall define materiality. In advancing in the other direction, we go toward a duration which stretches, tightens, and becomes more and more intensified: at the limit would be eternity. This time not only conceptual eternity, which is an eternity of death, but an eternity of life. It would be a living and consequently still moving eternity where our own duration

would find itself like the vibrations in light, and which would be the concretion of all duration as materiality is its dispersion. Between these two extreme limits moves intuition, and this movement is metaphysics itself. (CM 158)

As Deleuze picks up from this passage, Bergson's image of the cone, with its coexisting degrees of contraction and dilation, now applies to much more than just memory – it has been extended to the whole of the universe. Or put in the language of ontology: "This idea no longer simply signifies my relationship with being, but the relationship of all things with being. Everything happens as if the universe were a tremendous Memory" (B 77). From this we might surmise that duration has been pluralised, since everyone and everything seems to have its own particular duration. But this pluralism could be of two kinds: a 'generalized' pluralism, in which every duration is its own absolute; or a 'limited' pluralism, in which material things outside of ourselves are distinguished by the relative way in which they participate in our duration. Either way, these two would seem to stand in contrast to a monistic theory of time, in which there is only one duration. And yet it is this latter position that Bergson ultimately defends. To explain how Bergson ends up in this situation, despite his criticisms mentioned above, Deleuze draws our attention to Bergson's book *Duration and Simultaneity* – a text which aims to explain the relativity and totality of time in light of the findings of modern physics.

THE RELATIVITY AND TOTALITY OF TIME

How can it be that Bergson, the consummate thinker of multiplicity, comes to argue for a monism of time? Deleuze has a hypothesis for this: the cause is "Undoubtedly [Bergson's] confrontation with the theory of Relativity" (B 79). In the lead-up to his debate with Einstein in 1922 (see the Introduction of this book), Bergson intensely studied and reflected on the theory of Relativity – an encounter that culminated in the publication of

Duration and Simultaneity later that same year. Bergson, in a way, had no choice but to grapple with Relativity, for this revolutionary and powerful theory referred to all the same topics and notions that his own theory of time and space had been addressing. Bergson therefore realised the gravity of the situation: a failure to reconcile the results of Relativity with his own theories could be catastrophic.

As Canales tells us, Bergson and Einstein did not agree on much; indeed, their propensity to disagree on things – not only in the intellectual sphere but also socio-political issues – suggests that there was a personal edge to their animosity (Canales 2015: 8). Nevertheless, it must be stressed that it was not Bergson's intention to denounce Einstein. Bergson makes clear in *Duration and Simultaneity* that he does not wish to contest any of the scientific claims of Einstein's work. Bergson was also of the view, one could add, that the revolutionary findings of special relativity *confirmed*, rather than rejected, the philosophical positions that he had long been espousing (DS xxviii). Einstein's theory of special relativity, however, produced some well-known paradoxes debated by physicists – paradoxes that Bergson felt his theory of duration was able to resolve. Bergson thus did not disagree with the theory of relativity or its mathematical expression; rather he disagreed with the *interpretation* of the theory advanced by Einstein and the metaphysical implications surreptitiously involved. In Bergson's words: "In short, there is nothing to change in the mathematical expression of the theory of relativity. But physics would render a service to philosophy by giving up certain ways of speaking which lead the philosopher into error, and which risk fooling the physicist himself regarding the metaphysical implications of his views" (DS 145). Bergson's aim was thus to ward off such confusion and extemporise the metaphysics that Relativity deserved. As Deleuze says in the Afterword to *Bergsonism*: "This book [*Duration and Simultaneity*] led to so much misunderstanding because it was thought that Bergson was seeking to refute or correct Einstein, while in fact he wanted, by means of the new feature of duration, to give the theory of Relativity the meta-physics it lacked" (B 116; see also Čapek 1971: 238).

The significance of special relativity, simply put, stems from its abandonment of the Newtonian vision of space and time. For Newton, time is a unitary absolute that flows equably wherever it is found. Special relativity undermines this theory by arguing that the universe is more accurately "a multiplic-ity of physical systems of reference in motion relative to each other without absolute frame of reference" (Durie 1999: vi). This would appear to imply that there are "a multiplicity of times, a plurality of times, with different speeds of flow, all real, each one peculiar to a system of reference" (B 79). But if this is so, paradoxical situations, such as the 'twin paradox', can arise from their confluence.

Consider the following thought experiment. Paul takes a journey on a rocket into outer-space, rounding a distant planet before returning. All the while his friend Peter remains on earth. According to the Lorentz equations, upon which special relativ-ity is based, the clock in Paul's rocket will move at a slower rate relative to Peter's clock on earth. So when Paul finally returns and they compare clocks, the clock on earth will report a longer period of time than the clock on the rocket. It must be remem-bered, however, that the Lorentz equations hold regardless of whether the numbers are being crunched by Paul on the rocket or Peter on earth. This means that both of their clocks will appear to be slow when compared to the other. How, then, are we to make sense of this situation, where the multiple durations of Peter and Paul appear to be out of kilter with each other and the space-time that subtends them?[4]

Bergson's response is to say that of the multiple durations at play in this example only one of them is real, the others being imaginary. Peter, sitting on earth, exists in a time, t, that is con-temporaneous with his own duration. Meanwhile, Paul, who is strapped into his rocket, exists in another time, τ, that is con-temporaneous with his own duration. The Lorentz equations show that for Peter sitting on earth, τ is slower than t. However, 'τ relative to the earth', to borrow Durie's formulation, "is not a time which is contemporaneous with the duration of either observer" (DS xii). For as we established a moment ago, the time relative to the reference system of earth is t and the time relative to the reference system of the rocket is τ, so neither Peter nor Paul experience the time τ relative to the earth, or the time t relative to the rocket. What, then, is this 'τ relative to earth' or 't relative to the rocket' that the Lorentz equations speak of? They are *imaginary* or *fictitious* durations, lived by no one. They are *symbolic projections*, which demonstrate that the systemic reference point is given by the projector, not the system being projected. One could of course suppose that there is a larger system of reference that encapsulates the two relative systems of the earth and the rocket, but to do so would risk reintroducing the absolute of Newtonian space-time and run counter to the essential insight of special relativity. There is thus only one real time for Bergson, the time that is "lived or able to be lived" (DS 56), but this one real time is not the Newtonian absolute. While the Newtonian system admits to multiple real times on the grounds of a fictitious absolute, Bergson contends that there is only one real time and the rest are all imaginary or symbolic – a conclusion that he claims is confirmed by the fundamental insight of special relativity.

The perceptive reader will have noticed that central to Bergson's resolution is the element of Peter and Paul's 'own duration', as well as the assertion that real time must be lived or liveable. The conscious experience of Peter and Paul have thus become central in Bergson's account, and it is precisely this aspect of Bergson's theory that Einstein and his supporters criticise. For them, the physical reality of events has little to do with the manner in which they are perceived by conscious actors. The question then is: to what extent, if any, is the flowing of time dependent upon the consciousness of the perceiver? This can be addressed by asking an affiliated question: what is simultaneity, and when can we say that two events have occurred simultaneously? Imagine that a human being and some other kind of being, with faculties of perception that are vastly more attentive and sharp than the human, both observe two events occurring. To the human, these two events appear to occur at exactly the same time – simultaneously. For the other being, however, the two events are experienced as consecutive. Now imagine a third being, whose powers of perception are again of a different order, but this time in the other direction, so that events which appear to the human as separated by years are considered by this third being as simultaneous. What this tells us is that the determination of simultaneity depends in part on the nature of the consciousness that attends to the supposedly simultaneous events. Furthermore, the ascertainment of simultaneity may change from case to case, but in every case the events that are said to be simultaneous *must also be simultaneous with the duration of the consciousness that perceives them.* As the physicist will no doubt point out, humans have created instruments that are capable of measuring time at increasing levels of 'exactness'. Nevertheless, this does nothing to contest the claim that simultaneity at base is a *relative* determination, for regardless of how precise our instruments get it will always be theoretically possible to 'split' a moment in time. The determination of movement and simultaneity therefore finds its source in duration, with a special role played by *my* duration.[5]

The example that Bergson gives to demonstrate this consists of sitting on the bank of a river, watching the flow of the water and a bird fly over the water. The movement of the water and the movement of the bird are two distinct fluxes of motion; what brings them together in a system is me and my duration (the 'murmur of my life'), which is "the element that contains the other two" (B 80). As Deleuze goes on to say: "It is in this sense that my duration essentially has the power to disclose other durations, to encompass the others, and to encompass itself ad infinitum" (B 80).[6] We thus return to Bergson's thesis, most fully set out in *Matter and Memory* and rehashed in his "Introduction to Metaphysics". The insistence upon the centrality of my own duration is not to deny the existence of others, or suggest that the universe would cease to exist without observers; rather, it is to admit to the source of the sense of time – in a word, its *temporality*, which mathematical formulations cannot grasp. Special relativity, on Bergson's reading, dovetails perfectly with this account of time, because it shows that objective time is relative with respect to duration – a feature confirmed by the paradoxes discussed above, which are only paradoxical when the duration of the observer is ignored.[7]

Bergson's remarks about the paradoxes of special relativity, and his reminder about the importance of the 'lived' dimension of temporality, reprise a more well-known paradox that he resolved in his first book: Zeno's paradox of the race between Achilles and the tortoise. In this Ancient paradox, the Greek hero Achilles is in a footrace with a tortoise. The tortoise is given a head start so Achilles has some catching up to do. Being much faster than the tortoise, Achilles catches up quickly. But before he can take the overtaking step, it stands to reason that he must first cover half of that distance. By extension, before Achilles can take that half-step, he must first cover half of that distance, *ad infinitum*. Intellectually, it therefore appears that Achilles will never be able to overtake the tortoise, for every time he lunges to cover the last distance a prior task is placed before him.

Now, we of course know that Achilles must eventually be able to overtake the tortoise, so why then is there this perceived paradox? Bergson's answer has to do with the word 'step' or 'stride'. Every time we said that Achilles had only one more step to take, what we were referring to was a singular step, a stride, and this stride is a *qualitative whole* or *continuous multiplicity*. As such, it cannot be divided without changing it in kind. In other words, it is impossible to subdivide the 'stride' of Achilles without making it no longer Achilles'. If I was to join Achilles and the tortoise in their race, the spectator would expect that Achilles and I overtake the tortoise at different moments, as indeed we certainly would. We would do so at different parts of the race because my stride is a qualitative whole that *differs in kind* from Achilles' – it is mine, and only mine. The paradox arises when we presume that the three of us differ only in degree within the same unitary flux, when in fact we are three distinct fluxes; our strides comprise three different *durational contractions*. If I shared in the stride of Achilles, I would no longer be me – I would be Achilles. And reducing what is peculiar to our strides to some shared abstract substratum will not help matters, for it is indeed this fallacy that not only produces the paradox in the first place, but is also what motivated the development of special relativity. The paradox is thus overcome by remembering that each of our strides are something lived or liveable, and that they are three different durational contractions – continuous as opposed to discrete multiplicities. Put differently, Zeno's paradox can only ever arise *outside* of time, if duration is removed from the picture, or more exactly, reduced to space – time as the 'fourth dimension' of space. As Bergson explains:

> But the truth is that each of Achilles' steps is a simple indivisible act, and that, after a given number of these acts, Achilles will have passed the tortoise. The mistake of the Eleatics arises from their identification of this series of acts, each of which is *of a definite kind* and *indivisible*, with the homogeneous space which underlies them. As this space can be divided and put together again according to any law whatever, they think they are justified in reconstructing Achilles' whole movement, not with Achilles' kind of step, but with the tortoise's kind: in place of Achilles pursuing the tortoise they really put two tortoises, regulated by each other, two tortoises which agree to make the same kind of steps or simultaneous acts, so as never to catch one another. Why does Achilles outstrip the tortoise? Because each of Achilles' steps and each of the tortoise's steps are indivisible acts in so far as they are movements, and are different magnitudes in so far as they are space: so that addition will soon give a greater length for the space traversed by Achilles than is obtained by adding together the space traversed by the tortoise and the handicap with which it started. This is what Zeno leaves out of account when he reconstructs the movement

of Achilles according to the same law as the movement of the tortoise, forgetting that space alone can be divided and put together again in any way we like, and thus confusing space with motion. (TFW 113–14; see also CM 120–1)

Special relativity, in Bergson's opinion, provides the physics that correlates to his theory of duration and movement. At times, however, it runs into trouble when it fails to distinguish between the two multiplicities and treats space-time as a 'badly analysed composite'. Bergson's reading of Riemann's two multiplicities is therefore pivotal for dissolving the paradoxes of both ancient and modern physics. As Simon Duffy notes, it is often considered that Einstein was the first to recognise the significance of Riemann's ideas and put it to revolutionary work (2013: 105); however, if Deleuze is right then Bergson not only got there first – he also used Riemann to correct the interpretation of Einstein's work, insofar as the theory of multiplicities provides the means for showing how and why there is only one real time. Each flux is a virtual whole or virtual multiplicity, all of which are contractions of various degrees of a Totality that is their condition, in the same way that the various planes of memory were contractions of the virtual cone that is Memory. Time is thus not One in actuality, but *virtuality*.

So is time one or many, a single unity or a multiplicity of moments, absolute or relative? As we can now see, it is all or none of these things, depending on what one means by each of them. It is neither one nor many when these notions are posited as abstract contrarieties. Similarly, it is not a duration if by this term one means the dialectical synthesis of an immobile unity and multiple instants. Time is not an absolute in the Newtonian sense of this concept whereby it is uniformly and equably distributed. But it is also not relative, if by this term we mean that its movement is produced by the accumulation of innumerable states. On the contrary, time for Bergson is a virtual totality, which is to say a heterogeneous multiplicity. There are numerous durations – those of Peter and Paul, Achilles and the tortoise

– but these are disclosed by and accessed through my own lived duration, to which I have a special relation. Through intuition I am able to install myself in the movement of duration and thus gain an absolute rather than merely relative knowledge of it. But what this instalment opens me onto is the virtual whole that is Time – a virtuality coordinate with special relativity that is actualised in so many ways, as Peter watches his friend blast into the sky and I witness the footrace between Achilles and the tortoise.

Deleuze's own summation of the matter reads as follows:

> In short, from the first page of *Duration and Simultaneity* to the last, Bergson criticizes Einstein for having confused the virtual and the actual (the introduction of the symbolic factor, that is, of a fiction, expresses this confusion). He is criticized, therefore, for having confused the two types of multiplicity, virtual and actual. At the heart of the question 'Is duration one or multiple?' we find a completely different problem: Duration is a multiplicity, *but of what type?* Only the hypothesis of a single Time can, according to Bergson, account for the nature of virtual multiplicities. By confusing the two types – actual spatial multiplicities and virtual temporal multiplicity – Einstein has merely invented a new way of spatializing time. And we cannot deny the originality of his space-time and the stupendous achievement it represents for science. (Spatialization has never been pushed so far or in such a way.) But this achievement is that of a symbol for expressing composites, not that of something experienced that is capable, as Proust would say, of expressing 'a little time in the pure state'. Being, or Time, is a *multiplicity*. But it is precisely not 'multiple'; it is One, in conformity with *its* type of multiplicity. (B 85)[8]

FROM PURE DUALISM TO A NEW MONISM

Let us return to the supposed contradiction identified at the start of this chapter. Bergsonism, without doubt, is a dualistic philosophy, replete with all sorts of dualisms and a penchant to distinguish differences in kind. But beginning with *Matter and*

Memory and continuing through to *Duration and Simultaneity*, it would appear that Bergsonism has monistic ambitions, in which various differences in kind are encompassed within a whole as differences in degree – a situation summed up by the 'gigantic' cone of Memory and the Virtual Totality of time. Does this mean that Bergsonism is a monism and no longer a dualism? Some commentators have taken this to be Deleuze's reading, but things are arguably more nuanced than that.[9] Deleuze does not seek to choose one over the other. His aim is rather to explain how there is a "harmony between the dualism of differences in kind and the monism of degrees of expansion (*détente*), between the two moments of the method" (B 91). Far from discrediting dualistic interpretations of Bergson, Deleuze plainly states that "the moment of dualism has not been suppressed at all, but completely retains its sense" (B 91). So before we move on to explore the third and final stage of Bergsonism, a summary of the distinct 'moments' of Bergsonism, which comprise its 'progress', is in order.

As Deleuze sees it, there have been three 'moments of the method' thus far. (1) division of the composite; (2) balancing of the dualism; and (3) birth of a new monism. In Bergson's first book, *Time and Free Will*, he famously criticises those who confuse time with space. Time is poorly understood, he says there, because it has been inadequately distinguished from space, the two of which *differ in kind*. It is impossible to ever experience time or space on their own, since we always engage with them in mixture, but for this reason we must go *beyond experience* to articulate what is unique to each. The first moment of the method thus involves dividing or de-composing the composites given in experience. In this we are initially led by our senses, which is why Bergsonism is an empiricism, but the objective here is to go beyond them, which is why Bergsonism is a 'superior' empiricism. To achieve this Bergson instructs us to train our senses onto the actual *tendencies* or *directions* that make up a mixture. It is the division of these actual tendencies that Bergson is after, insofar as they point towards two pure kinds.

Hence why Deleuze refers to this first moment of the method as one of "pure dualism" (B 92).

In distinguishing differences in kind from differences in degree one is immediately confronted with a problem, which can be illustrated by the common language used to describe the two. When speaking of these two differences, for instance when explaining them to someone unfamiliar with Bergson, it is surprisingly difficult to *not* say that in Bergsonism there are two kinds of difference. Such a statement can't be quite right, since one of these two differences is 'difference in kind'. As Deleuze picks up, if Bergson's theory of difference is profound, it is not merely because he has said that we need to pay attention to differences in kind. Rather, it is because the two tendencies that he has separated out are the tendency to differ in kind and the tendency to differ in degree. In other words, what he has separated out are differences in kind, all of which reside on one side of the dualism, and differences in degree which reside on the other. For example, pure duration is not composed of differences in kind and differences in degree, and nor is space. Instead, duration "includes all the qualitative differences, to the point where it is alteration in relation to itself" (B 92) – that which differs from itself, or internal difference. Space, on the other hand, "only presents differences in degree" (B 92). The first moment of 'pure dualism' or division of the composite is thus followed by a second moment in which all of kind is grouped on one side and degree on the other – internal division on one side and external on the other. This moment of the method is still dualistic, but on Deleuze's description it is "the moment of neutralized, balanced dualism" (B 93).

So if we now have differences in kind, all residing on the one side, and differences in degree on the other, the obvious next question is: what is the difference between these two, one of kind or degree? How are we to understand this difference, and what is its relation to the two differences already laid out? This other or in-between difference, Deleuze says, is the Whole or totality of difference – that which encapsulates "all the *degrees of difference* or, in other words, the whole *nature of difference*" (B 93). Described in an image, it is the cone of Memory. As we know from that illustration, difference is incorporated in all of its degrees and kinds. Viewed from one perspective, each plane is a whole that is distinguished by how it differs in kind from all others; but when viewed from the other, each level of the cone is a degree of difference that has a number – the particular quantity of its radius, if you will. So within this cone, kind and degree, duration and matter, are all brought together into the one continuum:

> Duration is only the most contracted degree of matter, matter the most expanded (*détendu*) degree of duration. But duration is like a naturing nature (*nature naturate*), and matter a natured nature (*nature naturée*). Differences in degree are the lowest degree of Difference; differences in kind (*nature*) are the highest nature of Difference. There is no longer any dualism between nature and degrees. All the degrees coexist in a single Nature that is expressed, on the one hand, in differences in kind, and on the other, in differences in degree. This is the moment of monism: All the degrees coexist in a single Time, which is nature in itself. (B 93)

The three moments of the method thus move Bergsonism towards a monism, but we must be careful to note that this monism is not produced at the expense of dualism, as some kind of replacement or rejection of dualism. For starters, you don't get the monistic moment of Bergsonism without the prior moments of dualism. Their partnership, moreover, is not merely for methodological purposes, but is a key element in what is ultimately a *metaphysical* theory – a theory that aims to deliver precise knowledge in the field of metaphysics. Deleuze reminds us of this by drawing our attention to the actual and virtual dimensions of the different moments:

> For the duality was valid between actual tendencies, between actual directions leading beyond the first turn in experience. But the unity occurs at a second turn: The coexistence of all the degrees, of all the levels is virtual, only virtual. The point of unification is itself virtual. (B 93)

The suggestion that Deleuze would 'have done' with dualism thus clearly holds no water, for it would be akin to proposing that Bergsonism is a metaphysics of the virtual with no companion category of the actual.

This passage also provides a timely reminder as to *what* the totality of Bergsonism is, its ontological status: *it is the virtual*: "All the levels of expansion (*détente*) and contraction coexist in a single Time and form a totality; but this Whole, this One, are pure virtuality" (B 93).[10] So the totality of which Deleuze speaks is virtual, not actual – indicating once again the immense importance of the virtual/actual ontology to Deleuze's reading of Bergson. This virtual totality may be a Whole or One, but that doesn't mean it is undifferentiated or indivisible: on the contrary it is entirely composed of differences, in every which way. And neither is the Virtual a static entity in which 'all is given' in advance: on the contrary, it grows as time goes on, the growing of time itself, just as memory and the universe expand in time as time expands.[11]

One example that Deleuze mentions to explain these dualistic and monistic facets of Bergsonism is Bergson's treatment of intensity. As Deleuze notes in his early essays on Bergson, intensity is initially criticised by Bergson for covering over differences of nature with differences in degree, failing as a result to get at the internal difference of a thing in itself by being confined to distinguish between beings (B1 26 and BCD 37). On Deleuze's reading, however, this is not Bergson's last word on the matter: "The critique of intensity in *Time and Free Will* is highly ambiguous" (B 91). What he means by this is that Bergson's critique could be directed towards two different things: "the very notion of intensive quantity, or merely against the idea of an intensity of psychic states" (B 91). Deleuze's vote is for the latter, and his evidence is taken from *Matter and Memory*, where Bergson says that qualities are produced by the contraction of multiple vibrations, thus suggesting that "there are numbers enclosed in qualities, intensities included in duration" (B 92).[12] As this example of vibrations indicates,

115

intensities (as intensive quantities) lie *beneath* qualities – they coexist "in a dimension of depth" (B 92) and give rise to qualities, the former of which are *virtual* and the latter *actual*.[13] This claim does not contradict Bergson's critique of intensity in *Time and Free Will*, for what he specifically criticised there was the view that *psychic states* are intensities (as indicated by the title of chapter 1 "The Intensity of Psychic States"). For Bergson, psychic states are always already composites, so they will never solely correspond to a pure intensity. The commonplace understanding of intensity, in Bergson's terminology, is a 'badly analysed' composite because it fails to properly distinguish between degree and kind. But this critique does not mean that intensities have nothing to do with the experience of psychic states – in fact, they *produce* them: "If it is true that intensity is never given in a pure experience, is it not then intensity that *gives* all the qualities with which we make experience?" (B 92). So we see once again the significance that Deleuze places in the cone of memory and the dimension of depth that it alludes to – the *ontological*, as opposed to psychological, dimension. This image relies on and makes use of the dualistic tendencies of Bergsonism in aid of showing how the two sides are incorporated into a monism that contains all the degrees of difference (not merely differences in degree) and the whole nature of difference (not merely differences in nature). "This is why Bergson is not contradicting himself when he speaks of different intensities or degrees in a virtual coexistence, in a single Time, in a simple Totality" (B 94) – for there is all the difference between the virtual ontology of intensity and its manifestation in actual psychic states.[14]

We can now see why Deleuze would say that by "discovering a deeper contraction-memory at the heart of recollection-memory we have thus laid the foundations for the possibility of a new *monism*" (B 74). But in making this pronouncement we must not go too far: the dualistic tendencies of Bergsonism still remain – they still have their place, as it were, amongst the different moments and movements of Bergsonism (which is most likely why the monism of Bergsonism is referred to by Deleuze as 'new'). As Bergson will put it, a 'reconciliation' has occurred, alleviating the apparent contradiction of this theory:

> But, just because we have pushed dualism to an extreme, our analysis has perhaps dissociated its contradictory elements. The theory of pure perception on the one hand, of pure memory on the other, may thus prepare the way for a reconciliation between the unextended and the extended, between quality and quantity. (MM 236–7)

The impasse averted, we are now at liberty to continue to the third and final stage of Bergsonism – the *élan vital*. There we will find that Bergsonism has a fourth moment: the actualisation of the Virtual into lines of differentiation.

5

The Élan Vital *and Differentiation*

THE 'NEW DUALISM' OF BERGSONISM

It would be fair to say that chapter 4 of *Bergsonism* marks
the high point of Deleuze's reading. It is in this chapter that
he weaves together the various elements outlined in the previous three chapters and demonstrates how they lead to the
emergence of a 'new monism' – a monism that doesn't replace
or subvert the dualistic tendencies of Bergsonism, but rather
shows how they work in concert with the One or Whole that
is the Virtual. Bergsonism, however, does not end with the
announcement of this 'new monism'. Chapter 4 may be the
high point of *Bergsonism*, but it is certainly not the final point,
nor can it stand on its own or be 'the point' of Bergsonism, for
it does not go far enough. To the extent that the 'moment of
monism' is successfully laid out, this moment explains how the
universe, like Memory, forms a Virtual Totality; but the universe and our experience of it does not *actually* exist in this
manner. It follows that if we wish to understand the actuality
of the world and our experience of it then an appreciation of
the 'three moments' covered in the movement from dualism to
monism will not suffice: "A fourth moment must be added to
the three preceding ones – that of dualism recovered, mastered
and in a sense, generated" (B 94). Or as Deleuze puts it in one
of his earlier essays on Bergson: "Thus, if dualism is surpassed

119

in favor of monism, monism gives us a new dualism, this time mastered, dominated" (B1 27). The movement from dualism to monism is therefore followed by, of all things, a dualistic splitting of this monism.

The word 'new' in the above quote is extremely importantly, for the dualism that is being referred to is neither the 'pure' nor 'balanced' dualism discussed in the first two moments of the method. It is true that both the first and fourth moments involve the splitting of a unity into a dualism, but the unity and dualism in each case are very different. In the first case we started with a composite, such as the memory-perception mixture or space-time composite, that was then separated into its differences in kind through a process of virtualisation that extended actual tendencies beyond the turn of experience. In the second case, by contrast, we don't start with an actual composite or mixture but rather with the Virtual Whole, which is then divided into a dualism. So in both cases we arrive at a dualism, but the point we set out from is not the same, the dualism we arrive at is not the same, and the movement itself is not the same – in one instance we are moving from the actual to the virtual, while in the other we are moving from the virtual to the actual. Deleuze expresses it as follows:

> In both cases a dualism is established between tendencies that differ in kind. But this is *not* the same state of dualism, and *not* the same division. In the first type, it is a reflexive dualism, which *results from the decomposition of an impure composite*: It constitutes the first moment of the method. In the second type it is a genetic dualism, *the result of the differentiation of a Simple or a Pure*: It forms the final moment of the method that ultimately rediscovers the starting point on this new plane. (B 96)

According to Deleuze, the groundwork for this fourth moment has been prepared by *Matter and Memory*. In Deleuze's 1956 essay "Bergson, 1859–1941" he states that "the secret of Bergsonism is no doubt in *Matter and Memory*" (B1 30). What does he mean by this? Several things, each of which build on the previous. To begin with, we could say that the 'secret' of Bergsonism is *coexistence*: "Bergsonian duration is, in the final analysis, defined less by succession than by coexistence" (B 60). The reason this is a 'secret' is because it would appear to contradict the primary lesson from *Time and Free Will*, whereby duration is a successive flow in contrast to static spatial coexistence; but now with *Matter and Memory*, on Deleuze's reading, duration as a real succession *relies* upon virtual coexistence, in order for the present to pass. The development between these two books, however, is no mere inversion or reversal of positions, and the clue lies in the term *virtual*. The coexistence being espoused here is a virtual and not actual coexistence – a virtual coexistence of all the degrees of difference, rather than actual differences in degree. It is a 'Whole' or 'Totality' that contains 'all the degrees of difference', which is to say the 'whole nature of difference'. This brings us to the second reason for the elevated status of *Matter and Memory*: it is in this text that Bergson is able to reconcile the dualistic and monistic tendencies of Bergsonism – a programme that is "realized in *Matter and Memory*" (B 73). In attaining this unity, it is not as if monism 'wins out' over dualism; Bergsonism most definitely retains its dualistic traits and bases, which is why if the unity produced in *Matter and Memory* goes under the name 'monism' then it is better termed a '*new* monism'. But *Matter and Memory* does not conclude with the cone of Memory, since this theory would be rather meaningless without an explanation of how and why memories are actualised in different ways. Bergsonism is thus said by Deleuze to have a 'triple form': "We find the whole movement of Bergsonian thought concentrated in *Matter and Memory* in the triple form of difference of nature, coexistent degrees of difference, and differentiation" (B1 31). As this quote shows, 'coexistence' is only one form of difference in Bergson, and what it leads to is another. Bergsonism, moreover, does not consist in one or two of these forms alone, but demands an integrated understanding of all three, even if it is the second form that Deleuze takes to be the most profound (BCD 43–4).[1]

As we can now see, the 'new dualism' in question is more exactly the *process of differentiation*. This process is clearly not a 'one-off', nor is the 'new dualism' produced a singular set of terms or concepts, such as the dualism of differences in degree vs differences in kind. What the 'new dualism' rather refers to is an iterative process of dividing or splitting in two (which is one reason why Deleuze calls it a 'new' form of dualism). While all three forms of difference may be present in *Matter and Memory*, the texts that more fully explore the third form of difference as differentiation are Bergson's subsequent books *Creative Evolution* and *The Two Sources of Morality and Religion*. And the notion through which this process is pursued – the third stage of Bergsonism – is the *élan vital*.

THE DIVERGENCES OF THE ÉLAN VITAL

What is the *élan vital*? The *élan vital* – or 'vital impetus' when translated into English – is a notion first introduced by Bergson in *Creative Evolution*. It is a term used to help describe the nature of Life, and more specifically the nature of its movement, change and growth. As the reader will be well aware, by this point in his career Bergson has written extensively on the nature of movement, change and growth. It is therefore not surprising that at the centre of Bergson's investigation of life lies his notion of duration. Indeed, in the short introduction to *Creative Evolution* Bergson includes a footnote which says that this book will build on the findings of *Time and Free Will*, and in particular the notion of "real duration" which "signifies both undivided continuity and creation", in order to extend his theory of "psychical life" to "life in general" (CE xiv).

We will not rehash Bergson's theory of duration here, save to note that duration, on Deleuze's reading, is: (1) a heterogeneous multiplicity defined by the manner in which it differs from itself (i.e. the first form of difference);[2] and (2) a Whole that incorporates (via contraction) all the degrees of difference, which is to say the entire nature of difference (i.e. the second form of difference). Speaking to the first of these two points, Bergson reproached philosophers of time for repeatedly reducing time to space through a confusion of the two multiplicities and a failure to articulate a notion of *internal* difference, resulting in a notion of time devoid of temporality. This is why Bergson refers to his notion of duration as '*real* time' or '*real* duration'. In a similar fashion, what Bergson now hopes to achieve with his notion of the *élan vital* is to put the life back in Life – which is to say, articulate a notion of life adequate to the reality of life, to the *livedness* of life. Accordingly, Bergson implores us to approach life and our investigation of it *in duration*:

> [L]et us grasp afresh the external world as it really is, not superficially, in the present, but in depth, with the immediate past crowding upon it and imprinting upon it its impetus; let us in a word become accustomed to see all things *sub specie durationis*: immediately in our galvanized perception what is taut becomes relaxed, what is dormant awakens, what is dead comes to life again. (CM 106)

Bergson's philosophy of life therefore needs duration, and in a certain respect the *élan vital is* duration. As Suzanne Guerlac says: "The *élan vital* is an image for the process of time as duration" (Guerlac 2006: 7). Similarly, in the view of John Ó Maoilearca, Bergson's theory of life is "a theory of time generalised" (Ó Maoilearca 1999: 62). Or to quote Deleuze: "duration itself is an *élan vital*" (B1 28). But we must not go overboard here with our association between duration and the *élan vital*, for the two are not entirely identical. Deleuze makes this clear in his lecture course on Bergson's *Creative Evolution* (specifically its third chapter), which he delivered in 1960. After recognising that the philosophy of life needs a notion of duration to enliven it, Deleuze says that Bergson then "realizes that all his philosophy must become a philosophy of life, and duration must become the *élan vital*" (LC 21 March 1960). What does it mean, though, for duration to 'become' the *élan vital*? We should not think of this becoming as a transformation whereby one entity is replaced by another, in the way that we say 'the child becomes the man' (CE 312–13). Rather, "*The élan vital is duration that differentiates itself*" (LC 21 March 1960). The key here lies in the second form of duration-as-difference reprised above. The *élan vital* is *not* the Virtual Totality of Duration – *it is the actualisation of this virtual Whole along lines of differentiation*. "*Élan vital* would therefore be duration to the extent it is actualized, is differentiated. *Élan vital* is difference to the extent that it passes into act" (B1 28).

The *élan vital*, as such, cannot be synonymous with duration, for it is more precisely the process whereby the virtual Whole is actualised or 'acted out'; it is the force that pushes this process along. That being said, it is not as if the virtual Whole and its process of actualisation are associated with each other by mere chance – as we said before, the notion of Virtual Totality would be meaningless without a coordinate process of actualisation, and vice versa. In Deleuze's words, "it is the essence of the virtual to be actualized" (B1 28). The *élan vital*, therefore, is indeed duration, but it is more exactly the necessary actualisation of it, which is why Deleuze says that "*Creative Evolution* brings to *Time and Free Will* a necessary deepening as well as a necessary extension" (B1 28) – the *élan vital* is quite literally the extension of duration (and memory too for that matter) outwards, *fanwise*, through the process of actualisation along lines of differentiation. This brings into view the title of chapter 5 of *Bergsonism*: the *élan vital* is the *movement of differentiation*. What remains to be explained, though, is the nature of this movement.

Differentiation, as we have already noted, is dualistic in nature, but it is more accurately a plurality of dichotomous divisions, in which one split leads to two terms, each of which then undergo a further dualistic split, and so on. As Deleuze says: "Proceeding 'by dissociation and division', by 'dichotomy', is the essence of life" (B 94).[3] For instance: life divides into animal and plant; animal divides into instinct and intelligence while plant divides into the fixation of carbon or nitrogen; following one of the 'animal' lines, intelligence divides into the analysis of matter and the intuition of movement. Another way of framing this process is to say that life, for Bergson, is the *tendency to diverge*: "For life is tendency, and the essence of a tendency is to develop in the

The Élan Vital *and Differentiation*

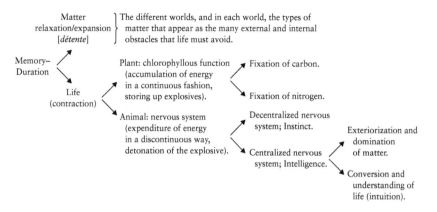

form of a sheaf, creating, by its very growth, divergent directions among which its impetus is divided" (CE 99). Or as Bergson will put it in his final book: "the essence of a vital tendency is to develop fan-wise, creating, by the mere fact of its growth, divergent directions, each of which will receive a certain proportion of the impetus" (TS 293–4). As these quotations suggest, Bergson's notion of 'tendency' plays a starring role in his theory of life. Bergson's aim, as we discussed in Chapter 1, is to distil the *actual tendencies* of a composite or whole. Tendencies are *directions of movement*, rather than static 'things', and it is only tendencies that can be said to genuinely differ in nature, rather than states of things. To this we can now add Bergson's claim that the essence of a tendency is to diverge, and that this is none other than the essence of life.

A controversial aspect of this theory is that life, from the perspective of Deleuze's Bergsonism, is *univocal*. On several occasions in *Creative Evolution* Bergson refers to the *élan vital* as an originary or universal force. This does not mean, however, that the *élan vital* is the same wherever it is found: on the contrary, it is different in each instance, as animal is different from plant and instinct from intelligence. It must be different, by necessity, otherwise there would be no division to speak of. There is thus an 'original impetus' to the *élan vital*, but it is the nature of this

125

impetus to divide and diverge, which is why it is found along different lines of differentiation. In Bergson's words: "We said of life
that, from its origin, it is the continuation of one and the same
impetus, divided into divergent lines of evolution" (CE 53).

Echoing such statements, Deleuze reports that "the *élan vital*
can be conceived as a unity: the movement of making itself"
(LC 2 May 1960). It is a unity, insofar as it is the Whole of
duration, but "it is in the nature of the *élan vital* and duration
to differentiate themselves" (LC 14 March 1960). The *élan vital*
is therefore the differentiation of duration: "Duration is differentiated within itself through an internal explosive force; it
is only affirmed and prolonged, it only advances, in branching
or ramified series" (B 94). Bergson evocatively describes this
process as proceeding "like a shell, which suddenly bursts into
fragments, which fragments, being themselves shells, burst in
their turn into fragments destined to burst again, and so on
for a time incommensurably long" (CE 98). The *élan vital* is
thus the explosive force that actualises the virtual unity of duration and univocal Being through a series of divergences: "It is
always a case of a virtuality in the process of being actualized,
a simplicity in the process of differentiating, a totality in the
process of dividing up" (B 94). And further:

> Why is differentiation an 'actualization'? Because it presupposes a
> unity, a virtual primordial totality that is dissociated according to
> lines of differentiation, but that still shows its subsisting unity and
> totality in each line. [. . .] Differentiation is always the actualization
> of a virtuality that persists across its actual divergent lines. (B 95)[4]

At this point in our analysis we must return to the footnote mentioned above where Bergson reminds us that "'real duration'
signifies both undivided continuity and creation" (CE xiv). By
now we have established that the movement of life and the *élan
vital* proceed by division and divergence. However, as the title of
Bergson's book plainly informs us, this movement is also most
importantly a *creative evolution*. How, then, is differentiation
creative, in the proper sense of this term?

THE CREATIVITY OF DIFFERENTIATION

Deleuze adopts a curious way of explaining the creativity of differentiation – he starts by returning to the question 'what is the nature of the Virtual?' The virtual has of course already been discussed at great length by Deleuze, principally in chapter 3 of *Bergsonism*. What Deleuze wants to bring our attention to now is the manner in which the virtual, on his reading of Bergson, differs from the notion of the possible. Deleuze asks: "How is it that, as early as *Time and Free Will*, then in *Matter and Memory*, Bergson's philosophy should have attributed such importance to the idea of virtuality at the very moment when it was challenging the category of possibility" (B 96)? As with the so-called 'strict rules' of Bergson's method of intuition discussed in Chapter 1, this statement about the importance Bergson places in the notion of the virtual must be taken with a grain of salt. There is no denying that Bergson's philosophy involves a novel and important use of the term 'virtual', but it must also be admitted that Bergson's use of the term throughout his works is not entirely consistent, and neither is it the case that the term is always used in contradistinction to the possible. In *Time and Free Will*, for example, the term only appears a handful of times, and at times as a synonym for the possible (see TFW 13). In *Matter and Memory* the virtual plays a more prominent part, most notably in the explication of 'pure memory'; but again, there are numerous instances where the term is contrasted with the real and used interchangeably with the possible as a projection of action – what Bergson calls "virtual action" (see MM 58, 168–9, 304 and 311). As for *Creative Evolution*, there are moments where the virtual is clearly distinguished from the possible in the manner described by Deleuze (see CE 293), however if the reader was to look up the word 'virtual' in the index of the English translation, they would find that the only entry of relevance – 'virtual action' – has one page reference and is cross-referred to 'possible action' (which has over a dozen page references).[5]

It is therefore clear that Deleuze is making more of the virtual than Bergson did, which is why it is a defining feature of Deleuze's reading of Bergson. This is most easily illustrated by Deleuze's capitalisation of the 'V' in Virtual – something that Bergson never did. When Deleuze employs a capital 'V' to spell the word it is to indicate that he is not merely referring to the 'virtual dimension' of reality, but more specifically to the Virtual Totality of duration, the gigantic and immemorial Memory, the unity of Time as a Whole, the whole of Nature or 'all the degrees of difference', the One that is said of the Virtual – in short, *THE* Virtual. When used in this manner, one could say that "The virtual has become a concept – a sort of *philosopheme*" (Guerlac 2006: 189). But while it is true that Deleuze has 'conceptualised' the virtual to a level not present in Bergson, the Virtual is not merely a philosophical concept: it is the ontology of reality. In addition, Deleuze does not use a capital 'V' each and every time he employs the term – such instances are in fact the minority. The point of importance here, as such, is not simply that the Virtual has become a concept in Deleuze when it wasn't in Bergson; of far greater significance is the elevated role that the notion plays in making sense of Bergson's thought and the inter-relation between its different stages. Thus if Deleuze makes of the Virtual a concept, he would no doubt maintain that it ultimately belongs to and has been produced by Bergsonism.

The place where Bergson certainly *does* focus his attention on these issues is his essay "The Possible and the Real", and it is this text that Deleuze's reading heavily relies upon. Bergson's use of the term virtual in that essay, however, *is the reverse* of Deleuze's. Let us therefore go back to the original before addressing Deleuze's subsequent explanation of the terms. Much of this story is already familiar to us, from our discussion of intuition as method in Chapter 1. There we saw how Bergson is interested in gaining 'precise' knowledge about our reality, not some abstract 'possible' reality. He therefore wants a theory that strictly corresponds to the facts of reality and does not embrace "all the possible, and sometimes even the impossible" (CM 50) – or, put differently, he is against those theories that embrace "all the real and all the possible" (CM 19). These comments from the two introductions to *The Creative Mind* are informed by his essay "The Possible and the Real", first delivered as a lecture at Oxford in 1920. Of the three examples given in this essay of 'nonexistent problems', it is the third that directly concerns the distinction between the possible and the real. A possibility, according to Bergson, does not precede its appearance in reality; rather, it is retrospectively posited. As Bergson famously says: "Backwards over the course of time a constant remodelling of the past by the present, of the cause by the effect, is being carried out" (CM 84–5). If this suggestion seems absurd, it is because the term 'possible' can be said in two different senses. Bergson explains it as follows:

> *Hamlet* was doubtless possible before being realized, if that means that there was no insurmountable obstacle to its realisation. In this particular sense one calls possible what is not impossible; and it stands to reason that this non-impossibility of a thing is the condition of its realisation. But the possible thus understood is in no degree virtual, something ideally pre-existent. If you close the gate you know no one will cross the road; it does not follow that you can predict who will cross when you open it. Nevertheless, from this quite negative sense of the term 'impossible' you pass surreptitiously, unconsciously to the positive sense. Possibility signified 'absence of hindrance' a few minutes ago: now you make of it a 'pre-existence under the form of an idea', which is quite another. In the first meaning of the word it was a truism to say that the possibility of a thing precedes its reality: by that you meant simply that obstacles, having been surmounted, were surmountable. But in the second meaning it is an absurdity, for it is clear that a mind in which the *Hamlet* of Shakespeare had taken shape in the form of possible would by that fact have created its reality: it would thus have been, by definition, Shakespeare himself. (CM 83)

Note how the word 'virtual' in the above passage has been aligned with the form of the possible that Bergson is criticising. This usage, furthermore, is consistent with the other three instances that the word is deployed in this lecture. Bergson's aim in discussing the possible and the real, to remind, is to show how there has been a confusion of the 'more' and the 'less'. In the case of the possible and the real, Bergson shows that there must be *more* in the possible than in the real:

> It is as though one were to fancy, in seeing his reflection in the mirror in front of him, that he could have touched it had he stayed behind it. Thus in judging that the possible does not presuppose the real, one admits that the realisation adds something to the simple possibility: the possible would have been there from all time, a phantom awaiting its hour; it would therefore have become reality by the addition of something, by some transfusion of blood or life. One does not see that the contrary is the case, that the possible implies the corresponding reality with, moreover, something added, since the possible is the combined effect of reality once it has appeared and of a condition which throws it back in time. The idea immanent in most philosophies and natural to the human mind, of possibles which would be realised by an acquisition of existence, is therefore pure illusion. One might as well claim that the man in flesh and blood comes from the materialization of his image seen in the mirror, because in that real man is everything found in this virtual image with, in addition, the solidity which makes it possible to touch it. But the truth is that more is needed here to obtain the virtual than is necessary for the real, more for the image of the man than for the man himself, for the image of the man will not be portrayed if the man is not first produced, and in addition one has to have the mirror. (CM 82–3)

Again we can see in the above that the word 'virtual' has been used as a synonym for the possible, and specifically the 'positive' sense of the term in which Shakespeare's *Hamlet*, as it were, has already taken shape before its realisation.[6]

So how does Deleuze interpret and use this text? Very well, if a little creatively. Although Bergson never uses the word 'opposition' or its like in "The Possible and the Real", Deleuze's reading revolves around two of them: the possible is the opposite of the real – it has no reality, it is lacking in reality; the virtual is not the

opposite of the real, it is opposed to the actual.[7] The virtual and
the actual are therefore both real, they possess reality, but different forms of it, one virtual and the other actual. The possible is
that which is 'realised', or more exactly, can be realised or not.
In other words, a possibility is something that is not real but will
either be realised or fail to be realised – one or the other – in the
same way that my hope of one day being rich enough to retire
will either be realised or it won't be. This relation between the
possible and the real is subject to two essential rules or principles:
"one of resemblance and another of limitation" (B 97). According to the rule of resemblance, the real and the possible are said
to *resemble* one another. As the conventional understanding of
possibility would have us think, there are innumerable possibilities laid out before us, one of which is then 'selected' in a process
of realisation. In this respect, the possible preexists the real, and
the two resemble one another – they look exactly the same, the
only difference being that the possible is an 'empty' or 'hollow'
version while the real is a filled in version of the same image.
Put differently, the real is the image of a possible with existence
added to it. As such, from the point of view of the concept there
is no difference between the possible and the real, for the image
of a possibility will look exactly the same as the real that takes
on that image when realising it. This movement from the possible
to the real is in turn guided by a rule of *limitation* or *elimina-
tion*, "by which some possibles are supposed to be repulsed or
thwarted, while others 'pass' into the real" (B 97).

In contrast to this, the virtual does not need to be realised,
since it is already real. Instead, the virtual becomes *actualised*.
The virtual cannot proceed by eliminating the possibilities before
it, for the virtual and the actual do not 'resemble' one another
as was the case with the possible and the real – the actual that
is actualised is not simply the same shape as the virtual it was,
with actuality added to it. For example, it wouldn't make much
sense to say that animal and plant 'resemble' life. The process of
actualisation is rather one of *differentiation*, whereby a virtual
unity diverges along different lines. Difference, as opposed to

the resemblance of identities, is thus primary in the process of actualisation: what is actualised are lines of divergence, lines of difference that differ according to the way in which differentiation occurs on each of them (similar to the different levels of the cone of memory). Furthermore, it is in this very act of diverging or splitting that the lines of differentiation are created in the first place. Lines of actualisation therefore do not preexist their reality, such as we find in the conventional schema of the possible and the real, but are created in and through the act of actualisation itself. We can then say that unlike the process of realisation, which obeys the principles of resemblance/identity and limitation/negation, the process of actualisation adheres to the principles of divergence/difference and proliferation/creation. As Deleuze concludes: "the characteristic of virtuality is to exist in such a way that it is actualized by being differentiated and is forced to differentiate itself, to create its lines of differentiation in order to be actualized" (B 97).

It is here that we get the connection between Deleuze's interpretation of the terms possible/real/virtual/actual and Bergson's theory of the evolution of life. The conventional conceptual framework of the possible and the real is incapable of adequately appreciating the *creative* nature of evolutionary developments, for it involves a conceptual presupposition of that which is created. Thus if an evolutionary process is to be genuinely creative as opposed to foreclosed, it will be necessary to employ the alternative framework of the virtual and the actual – or more specifically, the Virtual and its actualisations. "The impetus of life", Bergson says, "consists in a need of creation" (CE 251); and creation, according to Deleuze, is in need of the virtual/actual framework to ensure its creativity. This framework allows for the splitting or differentiation of the *élan vital* along lines of divergence, in which the 'result' of an evolutionary development does not preexist its emergence but rather unfolds in time. It therefore facilitates a truly *creative* evolution, for "*Time is invention or it is nothing at all*" (CE 341). It is true that the divergent lines actualised

132

"correspond to a particular degree in the virtual totality" (B 100), but "it should not be thought that the lines of actualization confine themselves to tracing these levels or degrees, to reproducing them by simple resemblance. For what coexisted in the virtual ceases to coexist in the actual and is distributed in lines or parts that cannot be summed up, each one retaining the whole, except from a certain perspective, from a certain point of view" (B 101). The creativity of evolution therefore belongs to the lines of differentiation themselves. In sum: "Evolution takes place from the virtual to actuals. Evolution is actualization, actualization is creation" (B 98).[8]

THE INDIVIDUATION OF THE ÉLAN VITAL

As the *élan vital* divides, it is propelled by the internal force of differentiation. In these actualisations, matter and the particular conditions of the environment are confronted and negotiated. Bergson refers to these instances as the solving of a problem. In one respect, each solution must be said to be a success, though always with respect to "the way in which the problem was stated, and the means that the living being had at its disposal to solve it" (B 103).[9] In other words, if the same solution is more developed in some organisms compared to others, we must still say that each is perfect with respect to their distinct conditions, in the same way as each level of the cone is "as perfect as it can be in varying degrees" (B 103). In another respect, however, not every solution in evolution can be deemed a success, and the history of evolution is littered with failed and semi-failed solutions. By definition, furthermore, every particular solution, insofar as it is peculiar to specific conditions, involves a retardation of the movement that invents it.

> Life as *movement* alienates itself in the material *form* that it creates; by actualizing itself, by differentiating itself, it loses 'contact with the rest of itself'. Every species is thus an arrest of movement; it could be said that the living being turns on itself and *closes itself.* (B 104)[10]

Thus if the movement of differentiation is a creative unfolding of the *élan vital*, it is no less a process of closure that produces individuated entities. In the same vein, life, on the one hand, proceeds by way of dissociation and division, but on the other hand it is equally the case that "Matter divides actually what was but potentially manifold [virtual multiplicity]; and, in this sense, individuation is in part the work of matter, in part the result of life's own inclination" (CE 258).[11] The diversity of life, in this respect, "depends on the manner by which matter resists the *élan vital*" (LC 2 May 1960). And as Deleuze concludes: "So, what is the origin of individuation? It is this resistance of a matter that is opposed to life" (LC 2 May 1960).

This closure of the *élan vital* in its confrontation with matter should not be seen as a bad thing, because without it nothing would be individuated and life as we know it would be impossible. For this reason Deleuze says that we should "be delighted that the *Whole* is not given" (B 104). Another way of putting this is to say that the closures of the *élan vital* are not foreclosed. The first chapter of *Creative Evolution* is in fact dedicated to making just this point. We cannot go into all of its details here, but in a nutshell Bergson sets up his philosophy of life in opposition to those accounts of evolution that adhere to either radical mechanism or radical finalism.

Radical mechanism holds that the evolution of life can be explained through an understanding of the mechanistic relations that determine cause-effect. Effectively Newtonian in predilection, it entails a vision of the universe that borrows heavily from the classical laws of physics and chemistry.

> The essence of mechanical explanation, in fact, is to regard the future and the past as calculable functions of the present, and thus to claim that *all is given*. On this hypothesis, past, present and future would be open at a glance to a super-human intellect capable of making the calculation. (CE 37)

As this quote suggests, for radical mechanism it is theoretically possible to use the knowledge of scientific laws to discover the movements of the universe in total. It may not be practically feasible to do so, but this is due to the incidental ability and limitations of our current technology and knowledge. Bergson agrees that the limitations of the human mind are a stumbling block, but for very different reasons. As we saw in Chapter 1, Bergson claims that the intellect naturally operates by fixating reality in order to analyse it. Because of this, mechanistic explanations "hold good for the systems that our thought artificially detaches from the whole" (CE 37), but for the same reason they are unable to properly appreciate the nature of change, including the movement of life. Mechanistic explanations undertaken by the intellect are hamstrung in particular by their overreliance on the past. The present is seen as being produced by the past, and by extension the future itself becomes nothing more than rearrangements and combinations of what already exists. Bergson does not deny that things such as plant and animal species arise due to specific causes, but what he rejects is the suggestion that these emergent entities can be adequately explained in advance by a mechanistic rationale; for if a new emergence is to be worthy of the name, it must be more than a mere rearrangement of the old, and thus irreducible to the past.

> [The intellect] instinctively selects in a given situation whatever is like something already known; it seeks this out, in order that it may apply its principle that 'like produces like'. In just this does the prevision of the future by common sense consist. Science carries this faculty to the highest possible degree of exactitude and precision, but does not alter its essential character. Like ordinary knowledge, in dealing with things science is concerned only with the aspect of *repetition*. Though the whole be original, science will always manage to analyze it into elements or aspects which are approximately a reproduction of the past. Science can work only on what is supposed to repeat itself – that is to say, on what is withdrawn, by hypothesis, from the action of real time. Anything that is irreducible and irreversible in the successive moments of a history eludes science. To get a notion of this irreducibility and irreversibility, we must break with scientific habits which are

adapted to the fundamental requirements of thought, we must do violence to the mind, go counter to the natural bent of the intellect. But that is just the function of philosophy. (CE 29)

We should be reminded here that by 'philosophy' Bergson specifically means 'metaphysics', which from its inception, on his view, has been concerned with exploring the nature of movement and change (CM 6 and 117). Science may wish to ignore philosophy, but insofar as it confines itself to the workings of the intellect, it precludes an understanding of 'real time' and thus evolution: "For time is here deprived of efficacy, and if it *does* nothing, it *is* nothing. Radical mechanism implies a metaphysic in which the totality of the real is postulated complete in eternity, and in which the apparent duration of things expresses merely the infirmity of a mind that cannot know everything at once" (CE 39).[12]

In contrast to radical mechanism, radical finalism is supple and amenable to reinterpretation, as it does not specify to the same level of exactitude what will occur at every moment in all facets. Rather, it simply insists upon the identity of what will be finally achieved. It is therefore a teleological doctrine that posits the programme to be realised. Radical finalism, perhaps even more obviously than radical mechanism, makes the existence of genuine creativity in the universe quite impossible. Worse than the notion of the 'possible' that Bergson will go on to critique, radical finalism purports to know in advance what will be realised, which is in turn used to explain the process leading towards it. The means by which it achieves this, however, is the same as in radical mechanism: the intellect, and its extrapolation from the known and the datum of the past forward into the unknown. The original purpose of thought, as Bergson established in *Matter and Memory*, is to inform and guide action. Human thought has no doubt gone beyond this immediate concern, for which we can be very grateful, but "Speculation is a luxury, while action is a necessity" (CE 44). Action, Bergson continues, involves the positing of an end (see Bergson's discussion of 'virtual action' in *Matter and Memory*), and the formulation of a plan to realise it. This plan is understandably based on what we know, which is based on our knowledge of what has occurred in similar circumstances. Repetition and our knowledge of mechanical causality thus directs radical finalism as it did radical mechanism: "Whether nature be conceived as an immense machine regulated by mathematical laws, or as the realization of a plan, these two ways of regarding it are only the consummation of two tendencies of mind which are complementary to each other, and which have their origin in the same vital necessities" (CE 45). Radical finalism, therefore, flounders in the same fashion as radical mechanism – through its inability to accommodate 'real time' or duration, which is a prerequisite for allowing creativity to be operative in the process of evolution.

> As in the mechanistic hypothesis, here again it is supposed that *all is given*. Finalism thus understood is only inverted mechanism. It springs from the same postulate, with this sole difference, that in the movement of our finite intellects along successive things, whose successiveness is reduced to a mere appearance, it holds in front of us the light with which it claims to guide us, instead of putting it behind. It substitutes the attraction of the future for the impulsion of the past. But succession remains none the less a mere appearance, as indeed does movement itself. (CE 39)

Given Bergson's critique of radical mechanism and radical finalism, does this mean he thinks that we can know nothing of what will occur in the future, that the future is entirely open and that everything is as equally likely to happen? Certainly not. For starters, what he is specifically criticising are *radical* versions of mechanism and finalism, insofar as they do not leave enough room for indeterminacy and the emergence of the new. Secondly, Bergson notes that his own position is finalistic, but of a certain kind: it is a finalism *with respect to the virtual whole*, as opposed to a finalism that allocates efficacy to that which is actualised.

THE FINALITY OF THE ÉLAN VITAL

This last comment requires some further fleshing out. Bergson contends that many radical finalists attempt to evade or "thin out" the implications of their position by "breaking [finality] into an infinite number of pieces" (CE 40). On the difficult question of whether matter or life has a final end they abstain from commenting or reject outright, but at the same time they entertain the suggestion that each organism taken separately has a finality and realises "a plan immanent in its substance" (CE 41). But as Bergson argues, this position leads to incoherent and arbitrary determinations, for within any organism there exist other elements that "may itself be an organism in certain cases" (CE 41). If the organisms living within another organism are subordinated to the finality of the 'larger' organism, then the 'smaller' organisms do not possess their own internal finality and are reduced to something external. It is therefore contradictory to maintain a theory of finalism that operates at the level of whole organisms and their supposed internal finality.[13] This means that if there is to be a kind of finality in nature, it must be one that coheres across life – a finality that is external to each individuated organism but internal to the Whole of life and its various dissociations. In Bergson's words:

> So it is of no use to try to restrict finality to the individuality of the living being. If there is finality in the world of life, it includes the whole of life in a single indivisible embrace. This life common to all the living undoubtedly presents many gaps and incoherences, and again it is not so mathematically *one* that it cannot allow each being to become individualized to a certain degree. But it forms a single whole, none the less; and we have to choose between the out-and-out negation of finality and the hypothesis which co-ordinates not only the parts of an organism with the organism itself, but also each living being with the collective whole of all others. (CE 43)[14]

Of this choice, Bergson prefers the latter option, and his reason for doing so can be summed up by the existence of the eye across numerous species, which is an instructive example given how extraordinarily complicated the apparatus is. An advocate of finality would argue that the single function, vision, coordinates the numerous parts to produce the eye. Initially this function will have been brought about by a slight development of the organ, which conferred an advantage, leading to further progressive actions and reactions between the function and the organ. Advocates of radical mechanism, as it happens, are not too far removed from this depiction, the difference being that they begin with the organ rather than the function. But rather than inquiring into the causal relation between organ and function, Bergson asks us to compare like-for-like organs, such as the eye of a vertebrate and the eye of a mollusc. The evolutionary split between vertebrates and molluscs, Bergson observes, occurred long before the first appearance of an eye. "Whence, then, the structural analogy?" (CE 62).

Darwin proposes that the emergence of an apparatus such as the eye is due to the accumulation by natural selection of slight and purely accidental variations, but Bergson is not convinced. Consider the evolution of an eye in an organism, whereby the organ changes over time and is improved in some way. The 'new' eye consists of several new developments (variations), but *when* do they arrive? One at a time, or all at once? Because Darwinian variations are 'accidental', it is hard to see why all of the variations required for the evolution would arrive at the same time. But if they arrive one at a time, then until the new eye has emerged the initial variations will not help the organism – indeed, they will most likely be a hindrance. It is therefore hard to see why the variation would be held onto, given that at this stage it contravenes the principle of natural selection. Innumerable other variations would also need to be 'held', since the organism cannot 'know' in advance which ones may become advantageous. The problems produced by Darwin's theory of 'insensible' variations are then multiplied when it is acknowledged that the eye has emerged on diverse and in some cases quite disparate lines of life. As Bergson asks: "How could the same small variations, incalculable in number, have ever occurred in the same order on two independent lines of evolution, if they were purely accidental? And how could they have been preserved by selection and accumulated in both cases, the same in the same order, when each of them, taken separately, was of no use?" (CE 64–5). This problematic situation, Bergson adds, is not alleviated by proposing that variations accumulate quickly leading to 'sudden' evolutions (as argued by William Bateson and Hugo de Vries). In this variant the 'holding' problem is lessened, but at the cost of coordination: "how do all the parts of the visual apparatus, suddenly changed, remain so well coordinated that the eye continues to exercise its function?" (CE 65) Again, this problem is amplified by the fact that the eye has developed on divergent lines of evolution. Thus as Deleuze summarises, "there would be no reason why the small successive variations should link up and add together in the same direction; nor any reason for sudden and simultaneous variations to be coordinated into a livable whole" (B 99).

A common response to this would be to say that it is the environment which does the work, determining the direction and coordination of the various excitations and variations. On this account, light is identified as the common cause of the development of the eye on several lines of evolution. To a certain extent Bergson agrees: the eye, Bergson will say, is a solution to the problem of light. But in what sense is the eye an evolutionary development that emerges as an adaptation to environmental conditions? The key word in this question, for Bergson, is 'adaptation', which can mean two different things:

We have already called attention to the ambiguity of the term 'adaptation'. The gradual complication of a form which is better and better adapted to the mold of outward circumstances is one thing, the increasingly complex structure of an instrument which derives more and more advantage from these circumstances is another. In the former case, the matter merely receives an imprint; in the second, it reacts positively, it solves a problem. Obviously it is this second sense of the word 'adapt' that is used when one says that the eye has become better and better adapted to the influence of light. But one passes more or less unconsciously from this sense to the other, and a purely mechanistic biology will strive to make the *passive* adaptation of an inert matter, which submits to the influence of its environment, mean the same as the *active* adaptation of an organism which derives from the influence an advantage it can appropriate. (CE 70)

As we can see here, Bergson does not deny that external environmental factors have an impact on the process of evolution. To admit to this, however, does not commit one to defending a mechanistic or accidental vision of biological adaptation and change. Moreover, advocates of the 'passive' theory, who would bestow agency on the 'outward circumstances' involved, covertly rely upon the 'active' meaning of adaptation as a positive reaction to a problem posed. As Bergson goes on to say, how "could light alone, a physical force, ever have provoked this change, and converted an impression left by it into a machine capable of using it" (CE 71)? The hypothesis is further damaged by findings in ontogenesis, which show that "parts differently situated, differently constituted, meant normally for different functions, are capable of performing the same duties and even of manufacturing when necessary, the same pieces of the machine" (CE 76). In such examples, "the same effect [is] obtained by different combinations of causes" (CE 76), which in turn contravenes the suggestion that the same effect – i.e. the eye on different lines of evolution – is produced in all cases by the same external cause (light). This theory of externally-led fabrication thus seems no less mysterious than that proposed by the gradual or sudden accumulation of accidental and insensible variations.

Insofar as external factors are incapable of giving us the full story, what will be required is an *internal* principle or *force* of development. This force, Bergson qualifies, is not the "effort of the living being to adapt itself to the circumstances of its existence", as proposed by Lamarck and Neo-Lamarckism (CE 77–8). Such individual effort, Bergson thinks, could never come close to approaching the level of effort required to effectuate an evolutionary change, even with the aid of hereditary transmission. Hereditary change is certainly related to a kind of effort, "but to an effort of far greater depth than the individual effort, far more independent of circumstances, an effort common to most representatives of the same species, inherent in the germs they bear rather than in their substance alone, an effort thereby assured of being passed on to their descendants" (CE 87). In a word, the effort of the *élan vital* – the internal force indigenous to the Whole of life.

> So we come back, by a somewhat roundabout way, to the idea we started from, that of an *original impetus* of life, passing from one generation of germs to the following generation of germs through the developed organisms which bridge the interval between the generations. This impetus, sustained right along the lines of evolution among which it gets divided, is the fundamental cause of variations, at least of those that are regularly passed on, that accumulate and create new species. In general, when species have begun to diverge from a common stock, they accentuate their divergence as they progress in their evolution. Yet, in certain definite points, they may evolve identically; in fact, they must do so if the hypothesis of a common impetus be accepted. (CE 87)[15]

The reason that the eye is taken as Bergson's preferred example, we noted earlier, is because the eye is an extraordinarily complicated apparatus. In attempting to explain its emergence and functioning, both radical mechanism and radical finalism pursue an *additive* line of reasoning: various elements are added together in order to explain how they eventually equate to the eye. Similarly, when it comes to appreciating its functionality, the eye is 'broken down' into its constituent parts in order to explain how the combination of these parts equates to the production of vision. When one reflects on all the miniscule components and the number of complex combinations that need to occur for vision to be produced, it would seem a miracle that it ever happened for one organism, let alone numerous disparate species. But Bergson argues that such a reflection views the eye from the wrong direction. For instance, consider moving your hand from point A to point B. There are innumerable points in space between A and B. If you were to reflect on how your hand needed to move between all of these sub-points, one after the other, and the level of coordination required to navigate between all these intermediary points, it would seem a miracle that your hand ever made it to B. This example should feel familiar, for it was the equivalent difficulty that Achilles faced when attempting to overtake the tortoise. As we saw there, the problem lies in viewing the effort through the lens of the *wrong multiplicity*. The eye is not a discrete multiplicity built up through the addition of components that differ in degree; rather, the eye is a qualitative whole, a continuous multiplicity (first form of difference). Moreover, it is itself part of a qualitative whole or continuous multiplicity, in the same way as the duration of Achilles and the tortoise are encompassed within Time as univocal Being or Difference (second form of difference). Therefore, if we wish to understand how the eye is individuated, we should not reflect on how it is built up through the addition of component parts that differ in degree; instead we must examine how the eye is *cut out of* the Whole through a process of differentiation (third form of difference): "*Life does not proceed by the association and addition of elements, but by dissociation and division*" (CE 89).

Bergson expands on this example by invoking the conceptual determinations of 'more' and 'less', which we discussed in Chapter 1. The movement of my hand from A to B, Bergson says, is *more* than the accumulation of the points passed through, for no matter how many points one envisions, no matter how close together and miniscule the points or elements are, they cannot account for the movement between them. There must therefore be some kind of effort or impetus beyond and through them. In another respect, however, the movement is *less* than the sum of the parts, in the same manner that the real is less than the possible. For aside from positing the conscious mind that segregates the movements into discrete parts, by subdividing the movement into an infinity of points one has converted what was once a simple arc into an assemblage of ever increasing components (with components within those components, *ad infinitum*). As Bergson describes in another telling example, if one were to imagine that a curve is produced by the coordination of innumerable sections of straight lines, ever smaller in length as our scientific powers of observation are improved, one would produce much useful knowledge but still never reach the true nature of the curve itself; one would also increasingly marvel at how so many tiny parts were able to work together to produce the curve.[16] As Bergson concludes from this:

> Just so with the relation of the eye to vision. There is in vision *more* than the component cells of the eye and their mutual coordination: in this sense, neither mechanism nor finalism go far enough. But, in another sense, mechanism and finalism both go too far, for they attribute to Nature the most formidable of the labors of Hercules in holding that she has exalted to the simple act of vision an infinity of infinitely complex elements, whereas Nature has had no more trouble in making an eye than I have in lifting my hand. (CE 91)

The fault or falsity of radical mechanism and radical finalism thus arises from their conceptual reliance on discrete multiplicities, and furthermore, the attempt to substitute increasingly complicated combinations of this multiplicity for a continuous multiplicity or multiplicity of fusion. All the while the 'intuitive' explanation lies elsewhere. The eye does not emerge from the addition of actualities, but through a dissociation of the *élan vital*, from the virtual to the actual. As Deleuze remarks, "Bergson criticizes mechanism and finalism in biology, as he does the dialectic in philosophy, for always composing movement from points of view, as a relation between actual terms instead of seeing in it the actualization of something virtual" (B1 28). How then do we explain the appearance of the eye on several different lines of differentiation? In each case, Bergson thinks, an effort is made in the direction of vision. As such there is a finality to the *élan vital*. But in each case the force comes from the one-and-only *élan vital*, differentiated and individuated in different ways – or more exactly, to varying *degrees of difference*. When we compare the eye of the eagle to that of 'lower' organisms, we will say that for the eagle's eye the *élan vital* has moved farther in the direction of vision, to a 'higher' degree. But each of these degrees are themselves a qualitative whole, like the different strides of Achilles and the tortoise; they are each 'all of a piece'. This is not to say that the eye of the mollusc is less perfect, for "all these organs, unequal as is their complexity, necessarily present an equal coordination" (CE 96). The stride of the tortoise, to finish the comparison, may not go as far as Achilles', but it is nonetheless equally well coordinated and perfect in its own way.

If there is a finalism in Bergsonism it is therefore a finality of direction or tendency, as opposed to a preconceived form to be realised or route to be taken. As for the nature of this tendency, the answer has already been provided: life is the tendency to diverge, which is to say that "life is, more than anything else, a tendency to act on inert matter" (CE 96). Precisely how it will act is not foreclosed, "hence the unforeseeable variety of forms which life, in evolving, sows along its path" (CE 96). Life therefore has a direction broadly speaking, but the way in which it is cashed out varies case to case, unfolding along different lines of differentiation, and it is in the act of each unfolding that each direction is gradually created. As Deleuze nicely sums it up: "There is finality because life does not operate without directions; but there is no 'goal', because these directions do not pre-exist ready-made, and are themselves created 'along with' the act that runs through them" (B 106).

We can now join with Deleuze in his outlining of the three requirements for Bergson's 'philosophy of life': (1) variations are not accidentally produced by external factors alone, but have an 'internal cause' – *internal difference*; (2) variations are not related to one another by association and addition, but rather

145

dissociation and division; and (3) "evolution does not move from one actual term to another actual term in a homogeneous unilinear series, but from a virtual term to the heterogeneous terms that actualize it along ramified series" (B 99–100).

THE HUMAN PRIVILEGE

Up till now our investigation of the third stage of Bergsonism has centred on *Creative Evolution*. In the last section of his book on Bergson, however, Deleuze extends his analysis to *The Two Sources of Morality and Religion*. These two texts are actually separated by 25 years, and in between their publication Bergson wrote *Duration and Simultaneity*. But on Deleuze's reading, *Creative Evolution* and *The Two Sources* are linked together by the notion of the *élan vital*. Put in simple terms, *The Two Sources* is an extension of Bergson's thesis from *Creative Evolution* into the realms of human society; so if *Creative Evolution* consists in the development of Bergson's theory of time into a theory of life, then *The Two Sources* consists in the development of this general theory of life into an analysis and theory of human society.

This concluding section of *Bergsonism* is brief (roughly six pages), but it is certainly not short on provocation. As Deleuze states in its opening paragraph: "[I]t is only on the line of [humanity] that the *élan vital* 'gets through'; [humanity] in this sense *is* 'the purpose of the entire process of evolution'" (B 106). What can it mean to say that humanity is the 'purpose' of evolution? Once again we must go back to Chapter 1 and the method of intuition. Recall how the aim of intuition as method is to take us "beyond the state of experience toward the conditions of experience" (B 27). Following the mathematical analogy of the curve, as we go 'around the bend' and out of sight, what comes into view is the Virtual; what we arrive at is the virtual point of intersection, where all the lines of difference converge to form the Whole or Totality that is the cone. The claim that Deleuze is now voicing is that of the various species of life, only humans are capable of rounding the bend to reach this virtual whole. This is to say that only humans are capable of going *beyond themselves.*

Such a claim has been implicit since at least *Matter and Memory* and is confirmed in *Duration and Simultaneity.* In the analysis of these texts we saw how Bergson was more than willing to admit to a plurality of durations – the various durations of other organisms and beings – but *my* duration was still granted a privileged status, as precisely that which disclosed the duration of others and proved that all are part of 'one' duration, a single Time. The intuition of my duration is thus the means by which I am opened onto life and durations beyond the human. As such, humans are a species that emerge on a line of differentiation, just like every other species do, and in this respect they exist in relations of equivalence with the rest of life as a certain degree of difference. But if humans are exceptional, it is because they are the only species with the means of grasping the Whole that they are degree of.

As Deleuze puts it, "[in humanity] the actual becomes adequate to the virtual" (B 106). And more expansively:

[Humanity] therefore creates a differentiation that is valid for the Whole, and [humanity] alone traces out an open direction that is able to express a whole that is itself open. Whereas the other directions are closed and go round in circles, whereas a distinct 'plane' of nature corresponds to each one, [humanity] is capable of scrambling the planes, of going beyond [its] own condition, in order finally to express naturing Nature. (B 107)

What is it that gives humans this unique capacity to go beyond themselves and grasp the virtual Whole? Deleuze doesn't actually mention the words, but the notion he relies on to address this question is the *zone of indetermination.* This notion is first introduced by Bergson in *Matter and Memory* when examining how images are selected by the brain. As we noted above, Bergson emphasises the centrality of action, and in particular 'virtual action', on determining thought and the formulation of plans. Perception, he says, means *eventual action*. A living being receives stimulation by matter and reacts to it according to how they might act in the world. For some 'rudimentary' organisms, this reaction is more or less immediate. For more 'complex' organisms, however, the interval between received excitation and eventual action is increased: "the reaction becomes more uncertain, and allows more room for suspense" (MM 22). In other words, the more complex an organism, the larger its zone of indetermination.

> By sight, by hearing, it enters into relation with an ever greater number of things, and is subject to more and more distant influences; and, whether these objects promise an advantage or threaten a danger, both promises and threats defer the date of their fulfilment. The degree of independence of which a living being is master, or, as we shall say, the zone of indetermination which surrounds its activity, allows, then, of an *a priori* estimate of the number and the distance of the things with which it is in relation. Whatever this relation may be, whatever be the inner nature of perception, we can affirm that its amplitude gives the exact measure of the indetermination of the act which is to follow. (MM 23)

In this discussion of matter stimulation, action and reaction it may seem that we are solely operating in the sphere of perception, but Bergson's radical claim, as we saw earlier, is that memory is also already in play. To repeat the key quote: "However brief we suppose any perception to be, it always occupies a certain duration, and involves consequently an effort of memory which prolongs one into another a plurality of moments. As we shall endeavour to show, even the 'subjectivity' of sensible qualities consists above all else in a kind of contraction of the real, effected by our memory" (MM 25). Because of this, "there is no perception which is not full of memories" (MM 24). In a way, therefore, the zone of indetermination is an interval into which the whole of memory descends and becomes actual (B 107). The zone of indetermination, we can thus say, is Memory.

Moving forward to *Creative Evolution*, the evolution of life is a process that effectively moves in the direction of increased complexity. As such, "at the root of life there is an effort to engraft on to the necessity of physical forces the largest possible amount of *indetermination*" (CE 114). This 'effort', as we know, is the *élan vital*. In this respect, the role of the *élan vital* is to "insert some *indetermination* into matter", to create what Bergson now calls "a veritable *reservoir of indetermination*" (CE 126). And as he further explains, the *élan vital* "is confronted with matter, [. . .] it seizes upon this matter, which is necessity itself, and strives to introduce into it the largest possible amount of indetermination and liberty" (CE 251). As we can now see, the zone of indetermination is not only memory, it is also synonymous with *freedom* – and the larger the reservoir, the more freedom the organism has in choosing how it reacts.[17]

It is on the line of humanity that this zone or reservoir of indetermination finds its greatest expression, its highest degree. In the human species, the *élan vital* has acted on matter to create an extraordinarily sophisticated apparatus of indetermination – human consciousness, as the 'knife' which cuts into matter, and its 'sharp edge', the human brain. As Deleuze puts it in his lecture course on Bergson, "the human brain, by its complexity, is a mechanism where the *élan vital* surpasses mechanism itself" (LC 9 May 1960). For Bergson "consciousness corresponds exactly to the living being's power of choice; it is co-extensive with the fringe of possible [i.e. virtual] action that surrounds the real action [and is therefore] synonymous with invention and with freedom" (CE 263–4). With human consciousness, the force of the *élan vital* has fashioned a "machine" or "instrument of freedom" that has facilitated the "triumph over mechanism" (CE 264). As such, the determinism of nature has been used to overcome the determinism of nature. Now, on the one hand, we might say that the difference between human consciousness and that of other animals is one of degree within the spectrum of life, in the same way that memory and perception form a monism. On the other hand, however, we must equally

General Diagram of Mechanism

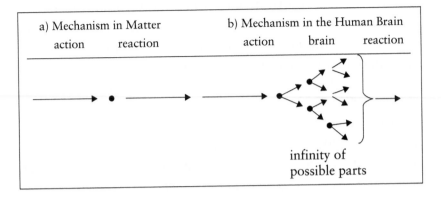

remember that just as the past and the present differ in kind, so too is there a "difference of kind, and not only of degree, which separates [humanity] from the rest of the animal world" (CE 265). Through the superiority of its brain, language and social life, the human alone has been able to overcome or *master* the matter out of which it is made: "[humanity] alone has cleared the obstacle" (CE 265).

It is for this reason that Bergson says humanity is the 'end' of evolution. This is said, though, in a very specific sense. Humanity is not the 'end' of evolution because it happens to lie at the end of the line, or because everything deterministically leads to it. The human does not emerge as the realisation of a pre-conceived or predetermined plan, nor can the rest of life be reduced to the human or retrospectively understood as existing "for the sake of [humanity]" (CE 265). Indeed, the human species could well have never emerged if the evolution of life had encountered an 'accident' that divided the *élan vital* otherwise. And it must also be noted that the human only exists on *one* of the many divergent lines of life, and in this respect is one of numerous different 'ends'. Thus if humanity is the "ground of evolution" (CE 266) it is in another sense. It is in the sense that the human is capable of *overcoming* determinism, rather than being mechanistically subject to it. It is in the sense that the human *transcends* the finalism of the *élan vital*, rather than being a preexisting point that life moves towards or a teleological plan realised. This is achieved because in the human species consciousness has been elevated to a level that its vital movement can be *continued indefinitely* (CE 266).

Note from this last sentence (and quotations above) that consciousness is not unique to the human. Other animals are clearly conscious, and in fact Bergson will extend the notion of consciousness beyond the animal kingdom to the entirety of life. Like the *élan vital*, consciousness is a whole that is actualised along various lines of differentiation in differing ways and to different extents. Bergson describes it as a "rising wave" that divides as it breaks on the shore, in its engagement with/in matter, leading to the individuation of life into distinct "souls":

> On flows the current, running through human generations, subdividing itself into individuals. This subdivision was vaguely indicated in it, but could not have been made clear without matter. Thus souls are continually being created, which, nevertheless, in a certain sense pre-existed. They are nothing else than the little rills into which the great river of life divides itself, flowing through the body of humanity. The movement of the stream is distinct from the river bed, although it must adopt its winding course. Consciousness is distinct form the organism it animates, although it must undergo its vicissitudes. (CE 269–70)

In the human, Nature has fashioned out of matter a brain in which consciousness becomes an 'intellect' capable of mastering matter – "the organ of domination and utilization of matter", as Deleuze describes it (B 108). However, although human consciousness is "pre-eminently intellect" (CE 267), "the destiny of consciousness is not bound up [. . .] with the destiny of cerebral matter" (CE 270). The human brain *intellectualises* consciousness by necessity, producing effects previously discussed (such as the spatialisation of time and the difficulty of grasping novelty), but the intellect represents only one of two directions in which consciousness moves, the other being *intuition*. While the intellect shares a natural affinity with matter, "intuition goes in the very direction of life" (CE 267). Intuition is only vaguely developed in the human species – as a "fringe", "nebula" or "halo" that surrounds intelligence (see TS 249–50, 268, 312) – and Bergson even entertains the hypothetical scenario in which life evolved differently to produce a human species with a different balance of intellect and intuition (CE 267). But things being as they are, the feeble light of intuition is nonetheless still able to shine through every now and then, illuminating the Whole of consciousness and life, in which "humanity no longer seems isolated in the nature that it dominates" (CE 270).[18] Also revealed in these "fleeting" moments is "the unity of spiritual life" (CE 268). Humanity is thus exceptional in the course of life, to the extent that it actualises consciousness in a manner capable of overcoming matter and also affords access to the virtual whole via intuition. Nevertheless, humanity is by no means isolated from nature and neither is it foreclosed. What makes humanity a part of the whole, moreover, is not simply that it is made out of the same material 'stuff' as the rest of the universe. This is certainly true, but of greater significance for Bergson is the 'spiritual' unity of consciousness – what Deleuze prefers to refer to as the Virtual – and the ways in which this totality is actualised in humanity.

In *The Two Sources*, Bergson extrapolates on this 'privilege' of the human. Building on the three superiorities listed above of the human brain, language and social life, Bergson now highlights the significance of humanity's sociability in relation to intelligence. What marks out the human, as we have seen, is the brand of its consciousness and complexity of its brain, which affords an elevated intellect and zone of indetermination. Social life also plays its part in storing and preserving the gains made by the *élan vital* in the human (CE 265). But although the sociability of humans cannot be achieved without the concomitant advancement of the intellect, sociability "does not derive from it" (B 108). This is to say that intelligence on its own is not responsible for humanity's grasping of the whole. In humanity, to put it differently, the vital movement

152

of consciousness can be continued indefinitely *in principle*, but this does not mean that it is in every instance of fact. On the contrary, relatively rare are the individuals that fully grasp the virtual whole – individuals that Bergson calls 'heroes' and 'mystics'. What, then, is it that marks out these "privileged souls" (B 111) from the rest of humanity?

Interestingly, it is not that they have a special affinity with intuition, for we already know who fits this characterisation: the philosopher. Instead, it is their relation to *emotion* that distinguishes the hero/mystic: "Only emotion differs in nature from both intelligence and instinct, from both intelligent individual egoism and quasi-instinctive social pressure" (B 110). Deleuze clarifies that the 'emotion' in question here is not something that is "connected to a representation on which it is supposed to depend" (B 110). What Bergson means to invoke is rather "the nature of emotion as pure element", an "essence" that is generative of new ideas (B 110). In this respect, it is emotion as *creative emotion* – creative "because it expresses the whole of creation, then because *it* creates the work in which it is expressed; and finally, because it communicates a little of this creativity to spectators or hearers" (B 110–11).[19] Creative emotion coincides with the whole of life, it is "a cosmic Memory, that actualizes all the levels at the same time, that liberates [humanity] from the plane (*plan*) or the level that is proper to [it], in order to make [the human] a creator, adequate to the whole movement of creation" (B 111). At its extreme, a society made up of such 'geniuses' would be the ultimate *open* society – a society, not unlike the notion of internal difference, whose nature is to change in nature. And a society devoid of such 'great souls' would be defined as *closed*, closer in kind to the societies of other animal species, which have a tendency towards consolidation (in reality, societies range somewhere between these two limits, as a mixture that is more or less open/closed in each instance).[20]

Bergson's thesis of the mystic, we must point out, is not at odds with his thoughts on philosophical intuition. It is more accurately a development and complexification of them (see TS 256–8). While Bergson attempts to encourage the philosopher to undertake the activity of intuition, he always stresses that the importance of doing so is due to the quite understandable, and in a certain respect natural, dominance that the intellect exerts when concerning matters of the mind. In place of contemplation, Bergson hopes to inject a little more creation in the activity of philosophy (B 111). The mystic, however, is further along the line towards pure intuition, where it is no longer "vague and evanescent" (TS 212) but concrete: "Everything happens as if that which remained indeterminate in philosophical intuition gained a new kind of determination in mystical intuition" (B 112). The philosopher may be "motivated by emotion" when conducting intuition as method, but it is the mystic who wholly encompasses creative emotion, and in so doing "gives, as it were, an envelope or a limit to all the aspects of method" (B 112). This is the moment "where the *Élan Vital* gains self-consciousness" (B 113) – the culmination, we could say, of the progress of Bergsonism as a whole.

Notes

INTRODUCTION

1. By the end of the First World War, twenty-one editions of *Creative Evolution* had been printed.

2. As Larry McGrath amusingly notes, the best-attended event of Bergson's visit to America was not even one of his public lectures: "More than a thousand showed up on February 20 to witness Bergson sipping tea with the wives of Columbia faculty" (McGrath 2013: 616).

3. Bergson's political career would continue after the Great War, most notably as the first president of the League of Nations committee that would become UNESCO. Other original members of this committee included Marie Curie and Albert Einstein.

4. In further recognition of the high esteem in which Bergson was held, in 1927 he was awarded the Nobel Prize in Literature. Only four other philosophers have ever received this award – Rudolf Eucken (1908), Bertrand Russell (1950), Albert Camus (1957) and Jean-Paul Sartre (1964).

5. Russell's entry on Bergson in this text is essentially a reproduction of an earlier 1912 paper, first presented to The Heretics at Cambridge on 11 March 1912, and published as "The Philosophy of Bergson" in volume 22 of *The Monist* (July, 1912), pp. 321–47.

6. In Russell's 'straw-man' reading, Bergson's philosophy is said to be guided by the dualism of instinct and intellect, "with instinct as the good boy and intellect as the bad boy" (Russell 1945: 793). For more on the intersection of Russell and Bergson see Durie 2004, Ansell Pearson 2002: 24–8, Canales 2015: 183–6 and Čapek 1971.

7. For an outstanding and comprehensive history of Bergson's debate with Einstein, see Canales 2015.

8. To give a better indication of its significance at the time, when Einstein received the 1921 Nobel Prize in Physics (which was held over to 1922), the prize was not awarded for his sensational work on relativity, but rather for his discovery of the law of the photoelectric effect. The reason for this, mentioned by the presenter of Einstein's prize at the awards ceremony, was that Bergson had raised doubts regarding the correct interpretation of Einstein's work on relativity. See Canales 2015: 4.

9. As many commentators have pointed out, the broad-brush accusation that Bergson was anti-intellectual or anti-scientific does not hold water (see, for example, Gunter 1969: v), as Bergson was both sympathetic towards and adept at scientific and mathematical thinking. In fact, before turning to philosophy, Bergson had aspirations to become a mathematician, and in 1876 he won a prize for his solution to a geometrical question found in a letter from Pascal to Fermat. Bergson's own response to his supposed anti-scientific bent was: "Where, when in what terms have I ever said anything of that sort? Can anyone show me, in all that I have written, one line, one word, which can be interpreted in this way?" (Bergson, cited in Grogin 1988: 127).

10. Other contributing factors, which should be mentioned in passing, include the observation that for the majority of Bergson's career he lectured at the Collège de France, which meant that he did not have students under his tutelage to develop into disciples, unlike university professors such as Edmund Husserl. Additionally, many of his papers were destroyed after his death by his wife (as instructed by his will).

11. For more on these connections see Durie 2002b, Kreps 2015, Čapek 1971, Gunter 1969 and 1991, and Prigogine and Stengers 1984.

12. According to Suzanne Guerlac, Deleuze alters his reading of Bergson from the mid-1950s to the mid-1960s, and again to the 1980s. In my view, while it is hard to deny that some elements of Deleuze's reading change through the decades (it would be somewhat strange if nothing changed) I would maintain that more remains the same than not. At any rate, I am unconvinced by the examples Guerlac provides. *Bergsonism* is said by her to be more 'systematic' than Deleuze's earlier essays, with the description

of 'intuition as method' in *Bergsonism* given as evidence (Guerlac 2006: 180). This assessment, however, overlooks Deleuze's 'other' 1956 essay, "Bergson, 1859–1941", which focuses from the outset on 'intuition as method' (this essay is not referenced by Guerlac). Guerlac also contends that the critique of the negative is "the single theme that most appeals to Deleuze in 1966", in turn making the themes identified in his 1988 Afterword to the English translation – intuition, multiplicities, and the relation of science and metaphysics – appear as a shift in position (see Guerlac 2006: 181 and 187). But it is not clear to me how she justifies this reading, seeing as these themes are very much present in Deleuze's *Bergsonism* (if not before) and feature to the same extent as the critique of the negative (if not more).

13. As Michel Foucault once famously said, "perhaps one day, this century will be known as Deleuzian" (Foucault 1977: 165)

14. By this I do not mean to suggest that all scholarship on Bergson after the publication of *Bergsonism* owes its origins to that text, since this is clearly not the case. Nevertheless, I would maintain that there is no greater influence than that of Deleuze's on the revival of Bergson studies. It is also telling that much of the best work published during the Bergsonian revival of the 1990s and 2000s bears the mark of Deleuze's reading. Regarding English-language publications I'm thinking in particular of the writings by Keith Ansell Pearson, Robin Durie, Leonard Lawlor, Elizabeth Grosz, Brian Massumi and Manuel DeLanda.

15. The other three listed are Heidegger's concept of being, Derrida's *différance* and Foucault's concept of utterance.

16. While no doubt an important text, few are the Deleuzians who would argue that the influence of Hume on Deleuze is in the same league as Bergson.

17. This mistake is likely due to a reliance on the publication dates of Deleuze's books (with *Bergsonism* fifth in line after books on Hume, Nietzsche, Kant and Proust). For further commentary on this issue see Alliez 1998: 227–8, Borradori 1999 and 2001, Gunter 2009, Ansell Pearson 2002: 201 and Guerlac 2006: 177. Also see Deleuze's infamous "Letter to a Harsh Critic", where he tells us how he came to Nietzsche after Bergson (N 6).

18. Although this point is debatable, I am not aware of any attempts to claim the converse, nor am I aware of any arguments that

convincingly establish the influence of Spinoza on Deleuze as a cut above Bergson.

19. In addition, it should be noted that Simondon himself is influenced by Bergson in various ways (see Chabot 2005).

20. Many commentators have claimed that Deleuze criticises and departs from Bergson's analysis of 'intensity', however as I have argued elsewhere (and again in this book), such an assessment is overly hasty and fails to properly appreciate the depth and complexity of Deleuze's Bergsonism (see Lundy 2017).

21. For a notable example of the former, of which there are many, see Grosz 2007: 287. For a notable example of the latter see Badiou 2000: 39. Although Badiou emphasises the centrality of Bergson for Deleuze, it cannot be said that Badiou accurately represents Deleuze's Bergsonism in this text, as pointed out by several scholars (see Widder 2001 and Ansell Pearson 2002: chapter 4).

22. While it is very difficult to reproach Gunter when it comes to his enormously important work on Bergson, his reading of Deleuze's Bergsonism is a different story. To mention just one instance, Gunter criticises Deleuze's treatment of Bergsonian method, "since it demotes thinking in duration to third place in the order of methodology" – something that is questionable for Gunter since "the problems involved in grasping duration *per se* surely came first in Bergson's thought" (Gunter 2009: 172). But this portrayal, in my view, misconstrues Deleuze's reading of method as intuition and the role that he sees it playing in Bergson's work. To begin with, the "fundamental meaning" of intuition as method, for Deleuze, is that "Intuition presupposes duration, it consists in thinking in terms of duration" (B 31). Secondly, Deleuze draws attention to two locations where Bergson explains how his method emerges from his investigation of duration (B 13). And thirdly, following on from the previous two, it would seem to me that the 'rules' of Bergson's method, as understood by Deleuze, must be taken 'as a whole' and are entirely interrelated in practice. Their order is thus not hierarchical or historical (who says that the third rule can't be the most important and/or have been operative from the outset?) and it is furthermore inaccurate to suggest that Deleuze has "displac[ed] duration from the centre of Bergson's thought" (Gunter 2009: 172).

23. According to Leonard Lawlor and Valentine Moulard-Leonard, "[Bergsonian] duration is the model for all of Deleuze's 'becomings'" (Lawlor and Moulard-Leonard 2016, section 7).

24. For more on the connection of Péguy and Bergson see my entry "Charles Péguy" forthcoming in the collection *Deleuze's Philosophical Lineage II* (Jones and Roffe, eds: forthcoming). Milič Čapek demonstrates a similar form of devotion when he says that Bergson erred in *Duration and Simultaneity* because he failed to fully grasp the implications of his *own* revolutionary thought: "the general theory [of relativity] not only does not conflict with [Bergson's] thought, but even agrees with the spirit of *Matter and Memory*" (Čapek 1971: 249). As this indicates, it is quite possible to affirm one's commitment to Bergsonism in the act of disagreeing with Bergson on a specific point.

25. It is occasionally said that Deleuze ignores Bergson's final book, *The Two Sources of Morality and Religion* (for one example see Frédéric Worms cited in Dosse 2010: 142). This is not entirely true, as Deleuze does deal with this text in the final section of his discussion of the *élan vital* and differentiation (and corresponding discussions can also be found in Deleuze's earlier engagements with Bergson). There is no denying, however, that the *Two Sources* features far less than Bergson's three other major books (each of which map onto one of the three stages of Deleuze's *Bergsonism*).

CHAPTER 1

1. Another early reader of Bergson who makes this point is H. Wildon Carr (see Carr 1919: 14).

2. Bergson, 1957–9, Vol. 3: 456. Deleuze refers to this quote on B 13.

3. Le Roy goes on in this passage to remark that: "We need plastic fluid, supple and living concepts, capable of being continually modelled on reality, of delicately following its infinite curves. The philosopher's task is then to create concepts much more than to combine them. And each of the concepts he creates must remain open and adjustable, ready for the necessary renewal and adaptation" (Le Roy 2015: 24). Le Roy is here drawing on Bergson's notion of 'mobile' or 'fluid' concepts, which he explains in his "Introduction to Metaphysics" (see CM 141 and 160). Readers of Deleuze will be aware that he too advocates a notion of 'mobile

concepts' and ultimately defines philosophy (in part) as the creation of concepts. As with Le Roy, therefore, it would appear that for Deleuze the original source of these views is Bergson.

4. See also MM 241: "This method [of intuition] presents, in its application, difficulties which are considerable and ever recurrent, because it demands for the solution of each new problem an entirely new effort." And see Bergson's "Introduction to Metaphysics", where he says: "But an empiricism worthy of the name, an empiricism which works only according to measure, sees itself obliged to make an absolutely new effort for each new object it studies" (CM 147).

5. As an aside, and in further response to his critics, Bergson argues that this confusion over clarity/obscurity explains why intuition might initially appear as philosophically inferior to intelligence. Describing a scene that will be familiar to most students of philosophy, Bergson says: "Listen to the discussion between any two philosophers one of whom upholds determinism, and the other liberty: it is always the determinist who seems to be in the right. He may be a beginner and his adversary a seasoned philosopher. He can plead his cause nonchalantly, while the other sweats blood for his. It will always be said of him that he is simple, clear and right. He is easily and naturally so, having only to collect thought ready to hand and phrases ready-made: science, language, common sense, the whole of intelligence is at his disposal. Criticism of an intuitive philosophy is so easy and so certain to be well received that it will always tempt the beginner. Regret may come later [. . .]" (CM 24).

6. To see where Deleuze takes this from Bergson, refer to CM 36.

7. As it happens, it is Althusser and his collaborators (in the *Reading Capital* project) that Deleuze mentions in this passage of *Difference and Repetition*. Althusser had also been working on 'the problematic' during this period, but one must not be misled into thinking that this is the source for Deleuze's own engagement. As I will establish, it is *through* his engagement with Bergson that Deleuze *first* starts to develop his own problematic philosophy. One might also note that in a letter written by Deleuze to Althusser in February 1966 – the same year *Bergsonism* would be published – Deleuze remarked that he was in the process of reading Althusser's books and wanted to say that he too had been working on "the concept of the 'problem'" (see Dosse 2010: 227). As this suggests,

the influence of Althusser and the 'French epistemological tradition' on Deleuze's 'problematic' thinking is ancillary.

8. Bergson's examination of false problems previously appears in *Creative Evolution*. See CE 178, 220–36, 274–7 and 296–9.

9. For further discussion of Bergson's "The Possible and the Real", see Gunter 2007.

10. See also Deleuze's 1956–7 lecture series *What is Grounding?*, pp. 114–16.

11. For a discussion of Deleuze's relation to the principle of sufficient reason in the context of Spinoza and Leibniz see Bell 2016: 3–7.

12. This notion of 'superior empiricism' will play a key role in Deleuze's later notion of 'transcendental empiricism'. See DR 57 and 143.

13. See also Deleuze's first published essay on Bergson: "What differs in nature is never a thing, but a tendency. A difference of nature is never between two products or between two things, but *in one and the same thing* between the two tendencies that traverse it, in one and the same product between two tendencies that encounter one another in it. Indeed, what is pure is never the thing; the thing is always a composite that must be dissociated; only the tendency is pure, which is to say that the true thing or the substance is the tendency itself" (B1 26).

14. For more on this issue see Sauvagnargues 2015: 48–50.

15. This manoeuvre of using one's own duration to go beyond oneself is a crucial aspect of Deleuze's reading of Bergson. Keith Ansell Pearson has written extensively on this issue and positioned it at the core of his own interpretation of Bergson (see Ansell Pearson 2002, 2005, 2007, 2010, 2015, 2016 and 2018). It is perhaps in this respect, more than any other, that Ansell Pearson's Bergsonism can be described as Deleuzian. I will delay further discussion of this aspect of Deleuze's reading to Chapters 4 and 5, for it is in these later contexts that the stakes are made more apparent.

CHAPTER 2

1. For more on this see Morris 2005: 282.

2. "Lettre à Höffding", in Bergson 1957–9, Vol. 3: 456.

3. In this exceptional article Durie covers many of the essential points and arguments of Deleuze's Bergsonism in condensed fashion. Durie also helpfully illuminates much of the surrounding

history of philosophy (for instance, the connections to Aristotle and Heidegger's work on time). The present text, while owing a debt to Durie's work, will consist in a more drawn-out explication led by the structure of Deleuze's book on Bergson and the 'whole' it comprises.

4. Deleuze will still hold this view when he comes to write the Afterword to the English translation of *Bergsonism* in 1988, remarking that "This is perhaps one of the least appreciated aspects of his thought – the constitution of a logic of multiplicities" (B 117).

5. My analysis here has stuck close to Deleuze's own explicit description in *Bergsonism*. For a fuller assessment of Riemannian manifolds in relation to Deleuze-Bergson see Durie 2004, Calamari 2015, Plotnitsky 2006 and Duffy 2013: chapter 3.

6. For Deleuze's earlier formulation of this see BCD 39, where he states: "In *Données immédiates*, we find the fundamental idea of *virtuality*, which will subsequently be taken up and developed in *Matter and Memory*: duration, the indivisible is not exactly that which does not allow itself to be divided; it is what changes its nature when it divides, and what changes its nature defines the virtual or the subjective."

7. See also Deleuze's first published essay on Bergson, where he states: "Being is alteration, alteration is substance. And that is what Bergson calls *duration*, because all the characteristics by which he defines it, after *Time and Free Will*, come back to this: duration is that which differs or that which changes nature, quality, heterogeneity, what differs from itself" (B1 25–6).

CHAPTER 3

1. For the corresponding point made in Deleuze's earlier work on Bergson, see B1 28: "Through all of its characteristics, duration is indeed memory because it prolongs the past in the present."

2. For the corresponding point made in Deleuze's earlier work on Bergson, see B1 24: "it is not the present that is and the past that is no longer, rather the present is useful; being is the past, being used to be". See also B1 29, which combines this point about 'being' and 'use' with the 'indestructible' nature of memories, previously mentioned, that 'preserve themselves': "The past does not have to survive psychologically, nor physiologically in our

brains, because it has not ceased to be, it has only ceased to be useful – it is; it survives in itself."

3. See Deleuze's earlier essay on Bergson, where he says: "The past is therefore the in-itself, the unconscious or more precisely, the *virtual*" (B1 29).

4. For Deleuze's earlier formulation of this point, see also B1 29: "The past is not constituted *after* it has been present; it *coexists with itself as present*. If we reflect upon it, we see that indeed the philosophical difficulty of the very notion of the past comes from the fact that it is in some way stuck between two presents: the present that it was and the current present in relation to which it is now past. The mistake of psychology, which badly sets up the *problem*, is to have retained the second present and therefore to have sought the past starting from something current, and finally, to have more or less situated it in the brain. But in fact, 'memory does not at all consist of a regression from the present to the past'. What Bergson shows us is that if the past is not past at the same time that it is present, not only will it never be able to be constituted, but it could also never thereafter be reconstituted starting from a later present. This, then, is the sense in which the past coexists with itself as present: duration is but this coexistence itself, this coexistence of itself with itself."

5. Bergson's understanding of habit is significantly influenced by his appreciation of Félix Ravaisson. See in particular his essay "The Life and Work of Ravaisson" in CM.

CHAPTER 4

1. Deleuze adds several references here, all taken from chapter 2 of *Matter and Memory*, which describe the "imperceptible stages" (MM 88) through which one passes in a "continuous movement" (MM 154) as "recollections take the form of a more complete, more concrete and more conscious representation" (MM 160).

2. See MM 76–7: "The qualitative heterogeneity of our successive perceptions of the universe results from the fact that each, in itself, extends over a certain depth of duration, and that memory condenses in each an enormous multiplicity of vibrations which appear to us all at once, although they are successive." See also MM 194: "In the fraction of a second which covers the briefest

possible perception of light, billions of vibrations have taken place, of which the first is separated from the last by an interval which is enormously divided. Your perception, however instantaneous, consists then in an incalculable multitude of remembered elements; and in truth every perception is already memory. *Practically we perceive only the past*, the pure present being the invisible progress of the past gnawing into the future."

3. For Bergson's earlier version of this analogy, see CE 31: "That life is a kind of mechanism I cordially agree. But is it the mechanism of parts artificially isolated within the whole of the universe, or is it the mechanism of the real whole? The real whole might well be, we conceive, an indivisible continuity. The systems we cut out within it would, properly speaking, not then be *parts* at all; they would be *partial views* of the whole. And, with these partial views put end to end, you will not make even a beginning of the reconstruction of the whole, any more than, by multiplying photographs of an object in a thousand different aspects, you will reproduce the object itself. So of life and of the physico-chemical phenomena to which you endeavor to reduce it. Analysis will undoubtedly resolve the process of organic creation into an ever-growing number of physico-chemical phenomena, and chemists and physicists will have to do, of course, with nothing but these. But it does not follow that chemistry and physics will ever give us the key to life."

4. My description of this example has relied on Robin Durie's introduction to *Duration and Simultaneity* (see DS ix–xi). Durie's astute explanation goes into greater detail than I will here, discussing important facets of the paradox such as the impact of the Doppler effect. My own treatment of the matter will limit itself to those aspects that are directly discussed by Deleuze, however I would recommend the reader to study the whole of Durie's introduction.

5. In his presentation at the Bergson Centennial event in Paris on 19 May 1959, Maurice Merleau-Ponty expands on this point, emphasising the role of perception in particular: "Today, as thirty-five years ago, physicists reproach Bergson for introducing the observer into relativistic physics, which, they say, can make time relative only with instruments of measurement or a system of reference. But what Bergson wishes to show is precisely that

there is no simultaneity between things in themselves, which, no matter how contiguous they may be, remain individuals. Only perceived things can participate in the same line of the present – and, in return, as soon as there is perception there is immediately, and with no other measurement, simultaneity of a single view, not only between two events in the same field but even between all perceptive fields, all observers, all durations" (Merleau-Ponty 1962: 139).

6. See DS 38: "It is therefore the simultaneity between two instants of two motions outside of us that enables us to measure time; but it is the simultaneity of these moments with moments pricked by them along our inner duration that makes this measurement one of time."

7. A most important text on this topic is Milič Čapek's *Bergson and Modern Physics: A Reinterpretation and Re-evaluation* (1971). In it Čapek contends that Bergson's assessment of the 'twin paradox' is correct, but only within the framework of special relativity and not general relativity (245–8). If Čapek is right about this, it may explain why Deleuze insists on the context of Riemann's theory of manifolds (and Bergson's awareness of it) for understanding the debate between Bergson and Einstein – as a way of correcting and improving Bergsonism, since the Riemannian context is necessary for appreciating general but not special relativity. In other words, Deleuze's placing of Bergson's argument within the Riemannian context ensures that Bergsonism is not dismissed or diminished in light of general relativity. As for Čapek, while he does not rely on the Riemannian context in the same manner as Deleuze, he nevertheless agrees that the means for correcting Bergson's error in *Duration and Simultaneity* can be found in Bergson's previous work (and indeed other parts of *Duration and Simultaneity*), concluding that "the general theory not only does not conflict with [Bergson's] thought, but even agrees with the spirit of *Matter and Memory*" (1971: 249).

8. For another explication of the issues discussed in this section see Ansell Pearson 2002: 55–65. Ansell Pearson follows Čapek in noting Bergson's error in *Duration and Simultaneity* (see Čapek 1971: 245–8 and my footnote above). Ansell Pearson also claims that Deleuze repeats the error, however he then goes on to ultimately adopt Deleuze's resolution of the debate, which turns on

the notion of the virtual in combination with Bergson's theory of multiplicities (such as I have just described).

9. See Kebede 2016: 116–17. Kebede's assessment suffers from a failure to appreciate the whole of Deleuze's Bergsonism – specifically chapter 5 of *Bergsonism*, which I will go on to discuss and in doing so demonstrate how Deleuze surpasses Kebede's characterisation.

10. See also B1 29: "We see therefore finally *what* is virtual: the coexistent degrees themselves and as such."

11. Deleuze includes an important footnote to justify his point: "According to Bergson, the word 'Whole' has a sense, but only on condition that it does *not* designate anything actual. He constantly recalls that: Whole is not given. This means, not that the idea of the whole is devoid of sense, but that it designates a virtuality, actual parts do not allow themselves to be totalized" (B 131–2, n.3).

12. In addition to the passages referenced above in footnote 2 of this chapter, see also MM 268–77, which discusses the issue at length, commencing with the question: "do real movements present merely differences of quantity, or are they not quality itself, vibrating, so to speak, internally, and beating time for its own existence through an often incalculable number of moments?"

13. Deleuze will also use the term 'beneath' (*sous*) in his first essay published on Bergson (B1 24).

14. For Deleuze's earlier formulation of this see BCD 49–50. Deleuze's reading of Bergsonian intensity will be crucial for his later work, in particular chapter 5 of *Difference and Repetition*. Although much of Deleuze's treatment of intensity in *Difference and Repetition* can be traced back to his earlier work on Bergson, there is only one mention of Bergson in this chapter. This reference, furthermore, appears at first glance to be a criticism of Bergson, since it opens with the statement that "the Bergsonian critique of intensity seems unconvincing" before recounting Bergson's critique of intensity in *Time and Free Will* (DR 239). But as the paragraph continues, Deleuze shows how intensity is recuperated by Bergson "in the great synthesis of Memory which allows all the degrees of difference to coexist as degrees of relaxation and contraction, and rediscovers at the heart of duration the implicated order of that intensity which had been denounced only provisionally and from

without" (DR 239). A footnote is then added which provides a highly condensed summary of the progressive stages of Bergson's triple form of difference and concludes by explaining how Bergsonism leads to "the reintroduction of intensities within duration, and the idea of a coexistence in duration of all the degrees of relaxation and contraction (DR 331, n.14). This clarification is worth mentioning due to the propensity of commentators to recite Deleuze's supposed criticism of Bergson on intensity without noting that the denouncement is *only provisional* and by no means the final word on the matter. The Bergsonian critique of intensity might *seem* unconvincing at first, but by the end of this paragraph in *Difference and Repetition* Deleuze has clearly affirmed the philosophy of intensity that Bergsonism as a whole has advanced – a position, I would furthermore point out, that is entirely consistent with Deleuze's stance in *Bergsonism*. See Ansell Pearson 1999: 74–6 and 2002: 214–15. See also Dan Smith's review of Ansell Pearson 2002, in which he admonishes Ansell Pearson for failing to emphasise Deleuze's supposed critique of Bergsonian intensity (Smith 2002). And for a fuller analysis of this issue see Lundy 2017.

CHAPTER 5

1. It is fairly common for scholars on Deleuze-Bergson to stress the thesis of virtual coexistence and rely heavily on Bergson's *Matter and Memory* for supporting material, reading Bergson's other work through this text (for a quintessential example see Al-Saji 2004; see also Ó Maoilearca 2004, which contains a critique of Deleuze's 'virtualism' that largely ignores those other parts of his Bergsonism which don't fit this narrative, such as chapters 1 and 5 of *Bergsonism*). This approach is legitimised by quotes from Deleuze such as those I have just referred to. Nevertheless, it is crucial, in my view, that this thesis of virtual coexistence be read and digested within the broader 'whole' of Deleuze's Bergsonism, in order to avoid lopsided appreciations of Deleuze's engagement with Bergson. In other words, the thesis of virtual coexistence cannot be taken to be the whole of Deleuze's Bergsonism, and it cannot be properly understood when isolated from the other 'stages' of Deleuze's Bergsonism and the method of intuition.

2. See Deleuze's short text on Bergson's theory of multiplicities, where he says: "For *élan vital* is like duration, it's neither one nor multiple, it's a type of multiplicity" (TMB).

3. For Deleuze's earlier formulation of this point see B1 28 and BCD 40: "dichotomy is the law of life". See also BCD 39: "Life is the process of difference."

4. See also BCD 40: "Virtuality exists in such a way that it actualizes itself as it dissociates itself; it must dissociate itself to actualize itself."

5. To those who would criticise Bergson for terminological inconsistencies, I would draw their attention to a remark by Fichte, which Bergson would most likely identify with: "I have sought so far as possible to avoid a fixed terminology – the easiest way for literalists to deprive a system of life, and make dry bones of it" (Fichte 1991: 90).

6. For the other appearance of the word 'virtual' in this essay see CM 79.

7. Deleuze says in this passage of *Bergsonism* that "We must take this terminology seriously" (B 96), but this comment should be taken as tongue-in-cheek, for it is Deleuze and not Bergson who clearly distinguishes between these four terms and injects them with conceptual rigour.

8. See also Deleuze's Lecture Course on chapter 3 of Bergson's *Creative Evolution*: "differentiation implies a virtual movement that actualizes itself – that is, a movement that creates at each instant two diverging lines" (LC 21 March 1960).

9. For the methodological import of this point, see my discussion of the first rule of 'intuition as method' in Chapter 1.

10. For Deleuze's earlier formulation of this point, see LC 21 March 1960: "The living is essentially a being that has problems and resolves them at each instant."

11. See also CE 251, where Bergson says: "The impetus of life, of which we are speaking, consists in a need of creation. It cannot create absolutely, because it is confronted with matter, that is to say with the movement that is the inverse of its own."

12. See also CE 340–1: "The painter is before his canvas, the colors are on the palette, the model is sitting – all this we see, and also we know the painter's style: do we foresee what will appear on

the canvas? We possess the elements of the problem; we know in an abstract way, how it will be solved, for the portrait will surely resemble the model and will surely resemble also the artist; but the concrete solution brings with it that unforeseeable nothing which is everything in a work of art. And it is this nothing that takes time. Nought as matter, it creates itself as form. The sprouting and flowering of this form are stretched out on an unshrinkable duration, which is one with their essence. So of the works of nature. Their novelty arises from an internal impetus which is progress or succession, which confers on succession a peculiar virtue or which owes to succession the whole of its virtue – which, at any rate, makes succession, or *continuity of interpenetration* in time, irreducible to a mere instantaneous juxtaposition in space. This is why the idea of reading in a present state of the material universe the future of living forms, and of unfolding now their history yet to come, involves a veritable absurdity."

13. In this passage Bergson criticises vitalistic theories for their adherence to theories of internal finality (see CE 42–3). It is very important to stress this point, as Bergson is frequently described as a vitalist and placed in the classical tradition of vitalism. Bergson is of course a vitalist thinker in one sense, as his notion of the *élan vital* indicates, but his vitalism is distinct from the tradition of that name, which his critique of internal finality demonstrates. For more on this see Durie 2002a: 371, Ó Maoilearca 1999: 97, and DiFrisco 2015: 54–6.

14. On Deleuze's reading of this point, see B 105: "The finality of the living being exists only insofar as it is essentially open onto a totality that is itself open."

15. See also CE 50: "each species, each individual even, retains only a certain impetus from the universal vital impulsion and tends to use this energy in its own interest".

16. See CE 31: "A very small element of a curve is very near being a straight line. And the smaller it is, the nearer. In the limit, it may be termed a part of the curve or a part of the straight line, as you please, for in each of its points a curve coincides with its tangent. So likewise 'vitality' is tangent, at any and every point, to physical and chemical forces; but such points are, as a fact, only views taken by a mind which imagines stops at various moments of

the movement that generates the curve. In reality, life is no more made of physico-chemical elements than a curve is composed of straight lines."

17. See LC 21 March 1960: "memory is a *function of the future*, for repetition consists in the forgetting of the past. More past = more future, and thus freedom." See also BCD 45: "In a different way than Freud, though just as profound, Bergson saw that memory was a function of the future, that memory and will were the same function, that only a being capable of memory could turn away from its past, free itself from the past, not repeat it, and do something new."

18. See also CE 270–1: "As the smallest grain of dust is bound up with our entire solar system, drawn along with it in that undivided movement of descent which is materiality itself, so all organized beings, from the humblest to the highest, from the first origins of life to the time in which we are, and in all places as in all times, do but evidence a single impulsion, the inverse of the movement of matter, and in itself indivisible. All the living hold together, and all yield to the same tremendous push. The animal takes its stand on the plant, man bestrides animality, and the whole of humanity, in space and in time, is one immense army galloping beside and before and behind each of us in an overwhelming charge able to beat down every resistance and clear the most formidable obstacles, perhaps even death."

19. See TS 53: "For heroism itself is a return to movement, and emanates from an emotion – infectious like all emotions – akin to the creative act."

20. For more on Deleuze's reading of Bergson's 'creative emotion', see Ansell Pearson 2015: 97–101.

Bibliography

Al-Saji, Alia (2004) "The Memory of Another Past: Bergson, Deleuze and a New Theory of Time", *Continental Philosophy Review* 37, pp. 203–39.

Alliez, Eric (1998) "On Deleuze's Bergsonism", *Discourse* 20:3, pp. 226–46.

Althusser, Louis (2006) *Philosophy of the Encounter: Later Writings, 1978–1987*, ed. François Matheron and Oliver Corpet, trans. G. M. Goshgarian. London and New York: Verso.

Althusser, Louis and Balibar, Étienne [1965] (1979) *Reading Capital*, trans. Ben Brewster. London: Verso.

Ansell Pearson, Keith (1999) *Germinal Life: The Difference and Repetition of Deleuze*. London and New York: Routledge.

Ansell Pearson, Keith (2002) *Philosophy and the Adventure of the Virtual: Bergson and the Time of Life*. London and New York: Routledge.

Ansell Pearson, Keith (2005) "The Reality of the Virtual: Bergson and Deleuze", *MLN* 120:5, pp. 1112–27.

Ansell Pearson, Keith (2007) "Beyond the Human Condition: An Introduction to Deleuze's Lecture Course", *SubStance* 114, 36:3, pp. 57–71.

Ansell Pearson, Keith (2010) "Bergson", in Dean Moyar (ed.), *The Routledge Companion to Nineteenth-Century Philosophy*. Oxford and New York: Routledge, pp. 403–31.

Ansell Pearson, Keith (2015) "Beyond the Human Condition: Bergson and Deleuze", in Jon Roffe and Hannah Stark (eds), *Deleuze and the Non/Human*. London: Palgrave Macmillan, pp. 81–102.

Ansell Pearson, Keith (2016) "Bergson's Reformation of Philosophy", *Journal of French and Francophone Philosophy. Revue de la philosophie française et de langue française* 24:2, pp. 84–105.

Ansell Pearson, Keith (2018) *Bergson: Thinking Beyond the Human Condition*. London and New York: Bloomsbury.

Ansell Pearson, Keith, Miquet, Paul-Antoine and Vaughan, Michael (2010) "Responses to Evolution: Spencer's Evolutionism, Bergsonism, and Contemporary Biology", in Alan D. Schrift (ed.), *The History of Continental Philosophy: Volume 3; The New Century: Bergsonism, Phenomenology and Responses to Modern Science*. Durham: Acumen, pp. 347–79.

Atkinson, Paul (2009) "Henri Bergson", in Graham Jones and Jon Roffe (eds), *Deleuze's Philosophical Lineage*. Edinburgh: Edinburgh University Press, pp. 237–60.

Badiou Alain [1997] (2000) *Deleuze: The Clamour of Being*, trans. Louise Burchill. Minneapolis: University of Minnesota Press.

Bell, Jeffrey A. (2016) *Deleuze and Guattari's* What is Philosophy?: *A Critical Introduction and Guide*. Edinburgh: Edinburgh University Press.

Bergson, Henri [1889] (2001) *Time and Free Will: An Essay on the Immediate Data of Consciousness*, trans. F. L. Pogson. Mineola, NY: Dover.

Bergson, Henri [1896] (2004) *Matter and Memory*, trans. Nancy Margaret Paul and W. Scott Palmer. Mineola, NY: Dover.

Bergson, Henri [1907] (1998) *Creative Evolution*, trans. Arthur Mitchell. Mineola, NY: Dover.

Bergson, Henri [1919] (2007) *Mind-Energy*, trans. H. Wildon Carr. Basingstoke: Palgrave Macmillan.

Bergson, Henri [1922] (1999) *Duration and Simultaneity: Bergson and the Einsteinian Universe*, ed. Robin Durie. Manchester: Clinamen Press.

Bergson, Henri [1932] (1977) *The Two Sources of Morality and Religion*, trans. R. Ashley Audra and Cloudesley Brereton. Notre Dame: University of Notre Dame Press.

Bergson, Henri [1934] (2007) *The Creative Mind: An Introduction to Metaphysics*, trans. Mabelle L. Andison. Mineola, NY: Dover.

Bergson, Henri (1957–9) *Ecrits et Paroles*. Paris: PUF.

Bibliography

Bianco, Giuseppe (2011) "Experience vs. Concept? The Role of Bergson in Twentieth-Century French Philosophy", *The European Legacy* 16:7, pp. 855–72.

Borradori, Giovanna (1999) "On the Presence of Bergson in Deleuze's Nietzsche", *Philosophy Today* 43, pp. 140–5.

Borradori, Giovanna (2001) "The Temporalization of Difference: Reflections on Deleuze's Interpretation of Bergson", *Continental Philosophy Review* 34, pp. 1–20.

Bowden, Sean (2011) *The Priority of Events: Deleuze's* Logic of Sense. Edinburgh: Edinburgh University Press.

Calamari, Martin (2015) "Riemann-Weyl in Deleuze's *Bergsonism* and the Constitution of the Contemporary Physico-Mathematical Space", *Deleuze Studies* 9:1, pp. 59–87.

Canales, Jimena (2015) *The Physicist and the Philosopher: Einstein, Bergson, and the Debate That Changed Our Understanding of Time*. Princeton and Oxford: Princeton University Press.

Čapek, Milič (1971) *Bergson and Modern Physics: A Reinterpretation and Re-evaluation*. Springer.

Carr, H. Wildon (1919) *Henri Bergson: The Philosophy of Change*. London and Edinburgh: T. C. and E. C. Jack.

Chabot, Pascal (2005) "The Philosophical August 4th: Simondon as a Reader of Bergson", *Angelaki* 10:2, pp. 103–8.

DeLanda, Manuel (2002) *Intensive Science and Virtual Philosophy*. London and New York: Continuum.

Deleuze, Gilles [1956–7] (2015) *What is Grounding?*, transcribed by Pierre Lefebvre and translated by Arjen Kleinherenbrink. Grand Rapids: &&& Publishing.

Deleuze, Gilles [1960] (2007) "Lecture Course on Chapter Three of Bergson's *Creative Evolution*", *SubStance* 114, 26:3, pp. 72–90.

Deleuze, Gilles [1966] (1991) *Bergsonism*, trans. Hugh Tomlinson and Barbara Habberjam. New York: Zone Books.

Deleuze, Gilles [1968] (1994) *Difference and Repetition*, trans. Paul Patton. London: Athlone Press.

Deleuze, Gilles (1970) "Théorie des multiplicités chez Bergson: une conference", at www.webdeleuze.com.

Deleuze, Gilles [1973] (2001) "Dualism, Monism and Multiplicities (Desire-Pleasure-*Jouissance*)", trans. Daniel W. Smith, *Contretemps* 2, pp. 92–108.

Deleuze, Gilles [1983] (1986) *Cinema 1: The Movement Image*, trans. Hugh Tomlinson and Barbara Habberjam. London: Athlone Press.

Deleuze, Gilles [1985] (1989) *Cinema 2: The Time Image*, trans. Hugh Tomlinson and Robert Galeta. Minneapolis: University of Minnesota Press.

Deleuze, Gilles [1990] (1995) *Negotiations: 1972–1990*, trans. Martin Joughin. New York: Columbia University Press.

Deleuze, Gilles [1993] (1998) *Essays Critical and Clinical*, trans. Daniel W. Smith and Michael A. Greco. London and New York: Verso.

Deleuze, Gilles [2002] (2004) *Desert Islands and Other Texts: 1953–1974*, ed. David Lapoujade, trans. Michael Taormina. New York and Los Angeles: Semiotext(e).

Deleuze, Gilles [2003] (2006) *Two Regimes of Madness: Texts and Interviews 1975–1995*, ed. David Lapoujade, trans. Ames Hodges and Mike Taormina. New York and Los Angeles: Semiotext(e).

Deleuze, Gilles and Guattari, Félix [1972] (1984) *Anti-Oedipus: Capitalism and Schizophrenia*, trans. Robert Hurley, Mark Seem and Helen R. Lane. London and New York: Continuum.

Deleuze, Gilles and Guattari, Félix [1980] (1989) *A Thousand Plateaus: Capitalism and Schizophrenia*, trans. Brian Massumi. Minneapolis: University of Minnesota.

Deleuze, Gilles and Guattari, Félix [1991] (1994) *What Is Philosophy?*, trans. Graham Burchell and Hugh Tomlinson. New York: Columbia University Press.

Deleuze, Gilles and Parnet, Claire [1977] (2002) *Dialogues II*, trans. Barbara Habberjam and Hugh Tomlinson. London and New York: Continuum.

DiFrisco, James (2015) "*Élan Vital* Revisited: Bergson and the Thermodynamic Paradigm", *Southern Journal of Philosophy* 53:1, pp. 54–73.

Dosse, François [2007] (2010) *Gilles Deleuze & Félix Guattari: Intersecting Lives*. New York: Columbia University Press.

Duffy, Simon B. (2013) *Deleuze and the History of Mathematics: In Defense of the 'New'*. London and New York: Bloomsbury.

Durie, Robin (1999) "Introduction" to Henri Bergson *Duration and Simultaneity*, ed. Robin Durie. Manchester: Clinamen Press.

Durie, Robin (2000) "Splitting Time: Bergson's Philosophical Legacy", *Philosophy Today* 44:2, pp. 152–68.

Durie, Robin (2002a) "Immanence and Difference: Toward a Relational Ontology", *Southern Journal of Philosophy* 40:2, pp. 161–89.

Durie, Robin (2002b) "Creativity and Life", *The Review of Metaphysics* 56, pp. 357–83.

Durie, Robin (2004) "The Mathematical Basis of Bergson's Philosophy", *Journal of the British Society for Phenomenology* 35:1, pp. 54–67.

Fichte, J. G. (1991) *The Science of Knowledge*, trans. Peter Heath and John Lachs. Cambridge: Cambridge University Press.

Foucault, Michel (1977) *Language, Counter-memory, Practice: Selected Essays and Interviews*. New York: Cornell University Press.

Grogin, Robert C. (1988) *The Bergsonian Controversy in France 1900–1914*. Calgary: University of Calgary Press.

Grosz, Elizabeth (2007) "Deleuze, Bergson and the Concept of Life", *Revue Internationale de Philosophie* 3, pp. 287–300.

Guerlac, Suzanne (2006) *Thinking in Time: An Introduction to Henri Bergson*. New York: Cornell University Press.

Gunter, P. A. Y. (1969) *Bergson and the Evolution of Physics*. Knoxville: University of Tennessee Press.

Gunter, P. A. Y. (1991) "Bergson and Non-linear Non-equilibrium Thermodynamics: an Application of Method", *Revue Internationale de Philosophie* 45:177, pp. 108–21.

Gunter, P. A. Y. (2007) "Bergson's Creation of the Possible", *SubStance*, 114, 26:3, pp. 33–41.

Gunter, P. A. Y. (2009) "Gilles Deleuze, Deleuze's Bergson and Bergson Himself", in Keith Robinson (ed.), *Deleuze, Whitehead, Bergson: Rhizomatic Connections*. New York: Palgrave, pp. 167–80.

Hyppolite, Jean (1962) "At the École Normale Supérieure", in Thomas Hanna (ed.), *The Bergsonian Heritage*. New York and London: Columbia University Press.

Iliadis, Andrew (2013) "A New Individuation: Deleuze's Simondon Connection", in *MediaTropes* 4:1, pp. 83–100.

Jones, Graham and Roffe, Jon (eds) (forthcoming) *Deleuze's Philosophical Lineage II*, Edinburgh: Edinburgh University Press.

Kant, Immanuel [1781] (2008) *The Critique of Pure Reason*. Radford, VA: Wilder.

Kebede, Messay (2016) "Beyond Dualism and Monism: Bergson's Slated Being", *Journal of French and Francophone Philosophy*.

Revue de la philosophie française et de langue française 24:2, pp. 106–30.

Kreps, David (2015) *Bergson, Complexity and Creative Emergence.* Basingstoke: Palgrave Macmillan.

Lawlor, Leonard (2003) *The Challenge of Bergsonism.* London and New York: Continuum.

Lawlor, Leonard and Moulard-Leonard, Valentine (2016) "Henri Bergson", *Stanford Encyclopedia of Philosophy*, at plato.stanford.edu.

Le Roy, Edouard [1912] (2015) *A New Philosophy: Henri Bergson.* London: Aeterna Press.

Lippmann, Walter (1912) *Everybody's Magazine*, Vol. 27.

Lundy, Craig (2009) "Deleuze's Untimely: Uses and Abuses in the Appropriation of Nietzsche", in Jeffrey A. Bell and Claire Colebrook (eds), *Deleuze and History*. Edinburgh: Edinburgh University Press, pp. 188–205.

Lundy, Craig (2012) *History and Becoming: Deleuze's Philosophy of Creativity.* Edinburgh: Edinburgh University Press.

Lundy, Craig (2013) "Bergson, History and Ontology", in J. Mullarkey and C. de Mille (eds), *Bergson and the Art of Immanence*, Edinburgh: Edinburgh University Press, pp. 17–31.

Lundy, Craig (2017) "Tracking the Triple Form of Difference: Deleuze's Bergsonism and the Asymmetrical Synthesis of the Sensible", *Deleuze Studies* 11:2, pp. 174–94.

Lundy, Craig (2018) "Bergson's Method of Problematisation and the Pursuit of Metaphysical Precision", *Angelaki* 23:2, pp. 31–44.

Lundy, Craig (forthcoming) "Charles Péguy", in Graham Jones and Jon Roffe (eds), *Deleuze's Philosophical Lineage II*. Edinburgh: Edinburgh University Press.

Lundy, Craig and Voss, Daniela (2015) *At the Edges of Thought: Deleuze and Post-Kantian Philosophy.* Edinburgh: Edinburgh University Press.

McGrath, Larry (2013) "Bergson Comes to America", *Journal of the History of Ideas* 74:4, pp. 599–620.

Marcel, Gabriel (1962) "At the Sorbonne", in Thomas Hanna (ed.), *The Bergsonian Heritage*. New York and London: Columbia University Press.

Marx, Karl [1859] (1993) *A Contribution to the Critique of Political Economy*, trans. S. W. Ryazanskaya. Moscow: Progress Publishers.

Massumi, Brian (1992) *A User's Guide to Capitalism and Schizophrenia*. Cambridge, MA: MIT Press.

Merleau-Ponty, Maurice (1962) "At the Sorbonne", in Thomas Hanna (ed.), *The Bergsonian Heritage*. New York and London: Columbia University Press.

Morris, David (2005) "Bergsonian Intuition, Husserlian Variation, Peirceian Abduction: Toward a Relation between Method, Sense, and Nature", *Southern Journal of Philosophy* 43, pp. 267–98.

Moulard-Leonard, Valentine (2008) *Bergson–Deleuze Encounters: Transcendental Experience and the Thought of the Virtual*. Albany: State University of New York Press.

Ó Maoilearca [previously Mullarkey], John (1999) *Bergson and Philosophy*. Notre Dame: University of Notre Dame Press.

Ó Maoilearca [previously Mullarkey], John (2004) "Forget the Virtual: Bergson, Actualism, and the Refraction of Reality", *Continental Philosophy Review* 37, pp. 469–93.

Péguy, Charles [1909–12] (1931) *Clio*. Paris: Gallimard.

Péguy, Charles (2001) *Temporal and Eternal*, trans. Alexander Dru. Indianapolis: Liberty Fund.

Perri, Trevor (2014) "Bergson's Philosophy of Memory", *Philosophy Compass* 9:12, pp. 837–47.

Piatti, Giulio (2016) "The Life and the Crystal: Paths into the Virtual in Bergson, Simondon and Deleuze", *La Deleuziana* 3, pp. 51–8.

Plotnitsky, Arkady (2006) "Manifolds: On the Concept of Space in Riemann and Deleuze", in Simon Duffy (ed.), *Virtual Mathematics: The Logic of Difference*. Bolton: Clinamen Press, pp. 187–208.

Prigogine, Ilya and Stengers, Isabelle (1984) *Order out of Chaos: Man's New Dialogue with Nature*. New York: Flamingo.

Riemann, Bernhard (1873) "On the Hypotheses which lie at the Foundations of Geometry", trans. W. K. Clifford, *Nature* 8:183.

Russell, Bertrand (1912) "The Philosophy of Bergson", *The Monist* 22 (July), pp. 321–47.

Russell, Bertrand (1945) *History of Western Philosophy*. New York: Simon and Schuster.

Sauvagnargues, Anne (2015) "The Problematic Idea, Neo-Kantianism and Maimon's Role in Deleuze's Thought", in Craig Lundy and Daniela Voss (eds), *At the Edges of Thought: Deleuze and Post-Kantian Philosophy*. Edinburgh: Edinburgh University Press, pp. 44–59.

Bibliography

Smith, Daniel W. (1997) "A Life of Pure Immanence: Deleuze's 'Critique et Clinique' Project", *Philosophy Today* 41, SPEP Supplement.

Smith, Daniel W. (2002) Review of Keith Ansell Pearson (2002) *Philosophy and the Adventure of the Virtual: Bergson and the Time of Life*, in *Notre Dame Philosophical Reviews*, 14 July 2002.

Wahl, Jean (1962) "At the Sorbonne", in Thomas Hanna (ed.), *The Bergsonian Heritage*. New York and London: Columbia University Press.

Wambacq, Judith (2011) "Maurice Merleau-Ponty's Criticism of Bergson's Theory of Time Seen Through the Work of Gilles Deleuze", *Studia Phænomenologica* 11, pp. 309–25.

Widder, Nathan (2001) "The Rights of Simulacra: Deleuze and the Univocity of Being", *Continental Philosophy Review* 34, pp. 437–53.

Index

absolute, 66, 99–100, 103, 105–6,
110–11
actual/actuality/actualisation, 8, 14, 25,
27, 38, 41, 57–60, 78, 79, 83, 85,
90–4, 97, 110–17, 119–21, 124–6,
131–4, 137, 144–8, 152–3, 166n,
168n; *see also* virtual
adaptation, 140–1
alteration, 65, 113, 162n
Althusser, L., 160–1n
aphasia, 93–4
Aristotle, 162
articulation
articulation of difference, 45, 64
articulation of the real, 37–40,
42–3, 48

Badiou, A., 158n
badly analysed composites, 34–7, 41,
71, 79, 110, 116
badly stated questions, 33–7, 163n;
see also problem/problematic/
problematisation
Bateson, W., 140
becoming, 11, 13, 123
the present as becoming, 75–6
being, 22, 27, 29, 31, 36–7, 101–3,
111, 126, 143, 157n, 162n
being and nonbeing, 33, 35–6, 61,
66–7
past as being, 75–7, 162n, 163n
see also order and disorder

Benda, J., 3, 11
brain, 39, 70–2, 147, 149–52, 163n

Camus, A., 155n
coexistence
coexistence of the past and the
present, 80, 88, 95, 163n
duration and coexistence, 87–9,
121, 163n
virtual coexistence, 15, 88, 90, 103,
114–16, 121, 133, 166n, 167n
see also past; virtual; whole
consciousness, 23, 73, 77–8, 81, 84–5,
100, 106–7, 143, 149–54
self-consciousness, 154
see also unconscious
contraction/*détente*, 70, 109–10,
114–15, 122, 167n
contraction memory, 82–3, 86–9,
98–9, 103, 116, 148, 166n,
167n
contraction of memory and
perception, 90–5, 98–9
contraction of vibrations, 98–9, 115

Darwin, C., 139–40
de Vries, H., 140
déjà vu, 80
Derrida, J., 157n
Dewey, J., 2
dialectic/dialectical, 6, 61–2, 64, 101,
110, 144

179